HOW WE
BEAT THE
ALL BLACKS

HOW WE
BEAT THE
ALL BLACKS

The 1971 Lions Speak

Edited by John Reason

This edition first published in Great Britain
2005 by Aurum Press Ltd
25 Bedford Avenue, London WC1B 3AT

First published 1972 as *The Lions Speak* by Rugby Books

A catalogue record for this book is available from the British Library.

ISBN 1 84513 145 2

1 3 5 7 9 10 8 6 4 2
2005 2007 2009 2008 2006

Designed and typeset in Bell and Kipp by David Fletcher Welch
Printed by MPG Books, Bodmin, Cornwall

CONTENTS

To the Tours Committee of the Four Home Unions, for their foresight and planning, which helped to make the 1971 British Isles Rugby Union tour of Australia and New Zealand such a resounding success.

THE TiGHT FORWARDS: THE SCRUM

By **Ian McLauchlan**

(Jordanhill College and Scotland)

My brief is to cover the front row and the second row, with particular reference to the scrummage. I shall deal more briefly with the role of the prop in the lineout and in the loose. And all this with particular reference to the Lions in New Zealand in 1971.

Scrummaging is a unit skill made up of various individual skills, each linked and interlocked into one efficient force. It is often difficult to pinpoint a weakness in a scrummage since it takes only one person not applying himself at the right time or in the right way to spoil what in all other respects could be an extremely good unit.

The scrummage is made up of ten men of different physical and mental characteristics and it was the recognition of these different characteristics and the application of greater technical knowledge that laid the foundation of the success that the Lions enjoyed in New Zealand.

I would like to talk about the front five in more detail under the headings of qualities (physical and mental), footwork and binding employed by these people within the confines of the scrum. Also the variations in technique used by the Lions in New Zealand to overcome what in many cases were physically huge packs.

Dealing first with the prop forwards, New Zealand in many ways did us a favour because they did not recognise that prop forward is a very specialised position. They had ignored the primary duties of a prop which is in the confines of a scrummage and had rather given him his secondary function which in their case was jumping at number two in the lineout and running about in the loose. The failure to recognise the importance of the position

1

led them to putting in men who were physically very, very big and who were technically very, very poor. They lost out because they came up against technical experts and were destroyed!

New Zealanders had no room for a small man in their teams. They always picked big and they lost because in many games they played flankers or locks in the front row. These men had no idea of the pressure that was going to be put on them or how to offset this pressure.

Qualities required

It goes without saying that at the top level, all tight forwards must be very strong. They must have great general strength and if I had to pick out any particular strength, I would say that this must be in the legs. A tight forward must have strong legs to be a good scrummager.

These men must also have great stamina, because they must fulfil their function as scrummagers and become ball winners in the loose as well as play their part in attack from the lineout.

Mentally, props must be hard. This is particularly true of the loose head because he is responsible for defending his own put-in and therefore cannot afford to be messed about. Admittedly, this applies to all members of the front row, but the loose head has a double job. He has to protect his hooker against boring or lowering and he has to help win his own ball.

The mental pressure on a tight head prop is not so great, because he is not defending his own ball and any ball he does win against the head is counted as a bonus.

The mental attitude of props must be uncompromising because they are in immediate contact with the opposition and the least sign of weakness will be exploited by experienced opponents.

In New Zealand, where forward domination is so much a part of the game, this mental as well as physical hardness is very necessary. The capacity to absorb hard knocks is not enough, and everybody in the Lions' front five had to show themselves capable of handing out punishment as well as absorbing it. Failure to retaliate immediately was interpreted as a sign of weakness.

I want to stress that any player who is going to be a success in the front five of a scrum must accept that this is an unglamorous position. He must accept that the donkey work has to be done first and that it has to be done well for the rest of his team to play well. Anything that a prop does apart from that donkey work is a bonus, and with the demands as they are at the moment, those bonuses are becoming harder to find.

Body positions of props and locks in the scrum

Props must remain square at all times. Any twisting or lowering of the body weakens their own position and subsequently weakens the ability of the other players in the scrummage to apply and to bear weight. I believe that the angling of the body inwards by the tight head causes most of the scrummage collapsing which has become a feature of top level rugby in recent seasons. It is also a cause of many rib injuries to props. The body should be square and the back flat since the flat back is the only method by which you can transfer power efficiently and resist the weight of the opposition. Any rounding of the back is an indication of poor technique or compensation for the fact that the player is not really strong enough to fill the position.

The errors in technique can be easily corrected by a coach. The lack of strength is up to the individual concerned and takes longer to remedy.

Tight forwards should force their heads upwards in the scrummage so that as little weight as possible is borne by the neck. Pressure on the neck forces a prop to bend and twist.

The height at which the two props scrummage depends on the hooker's tastes, but generally the loose head should be higher than the tight head on his own ball and lower on the opposition ball.

Footwork

Coaching manuals usually refer to three different foot placements for the props, but at the top level, I have only come across two of them.

The first method is for both the tight head and loose head props to scrummage with the outside foot forward and the inside foot back. On his own ball, the loose head stands with his right foot almost directly behind his left. This allows a channel through which the ball can pass and it also allows the hooker to come across.

The method used by the shorter legged members of the front row is to stand with the legs astride with the right leg slightly back so that the hooker sits in the space in front of the loose head's right thigh. This brings the hooker much nearer the mouth of the tunnel and cuts down the chance of losing his own ball.

The third variation of foot placement is for the props to stand with their inside feet up and their outside feet back. I have read about this but I have never tried it myself and I have never seen anybody else try it. The theory behind it is that it keeps the front row together, but I always thought that is what your arms are for.

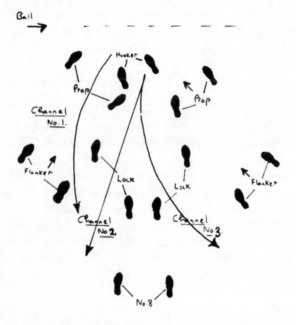

Scrummage foot positions for ball with the head.
The hooker is half-turned and sitting in front of the right thigh of his loose head prop. The hooker can then put downward pressure on his opponent with his right shoulder. The hooker using his left foot need not move so far across but this sort of strike makes a good channel difficult.

At all times, the props should be pushing slightly inwards and forwards to keep the front row tight as a unit.

The footwork of the locks is similar to that of the props. They all scrummage with their outside foot forward and their inside foot back. I have never seen any locks scrummage with their inside feet forward and their outside feet back, even though you can find it suggested in coaching manuals.

THE HOOKER

This is a separate position and a specialist one. The hoooker is traditionally the smallest member of the pack with the sharpest wits. He needs to be nimble as well as strong. He has to operate in a very limited space. His reactions must be sharp and he must also have the stamina to contribute to ball winning in the loose.

BODY POSITION

On his own ball, the hooker will push down with his right shoulder to pressurise his opponent and to try to edge him away from the ball. This helps to create space in which to work.

Against the head, the hooker's right shoulder will be pushing hard on his opponent's neck to try to weigh him down and to make it as difficult as possible for him to strike for the ball.

BINDING

Briefly, the tighter the better, but most hookers vary their binding in different situations. The most popular is for the hooker to bind with his arms over the shoulders of his props on his own ball so that he is up ahead of his props and also bearing weight on his opponent. This keeps the front row together and avoids the loose head splitting away from his hooker. It also gives slightly more space in which to work and at the same time it allows the loose head to come closer and to take more weight off the opposing tight head.

If the opposing tight head is exerting pressure, the hooker may find it a help to bind under the shoulder of his loose head. This allows the loose head to move forward and take more of the weight being applied by the opposing tight head.

Against the head, most hookers bind over the tight head and under the loose head. This allows a certain movement within the scrum while preserving a tight binding. It also enables the hooker to drop his right shoulder and bear down on his opponent.

Underbinding is very rarely used in this country, although it is often used in the Argentine. It makes it difficult to put pressure on the hooker, but against that, it asks a lot of the props because it puts extra pressure on them. It does allow the hooker to move very freely and it does help near-foot strikers on their own ball.

It was in the binding that the greatest difference lay between the Lions and New Zealand packs. The Lions' binding was always very tight. That of many of the New Zealand packs wasn't. Consequently, their scrums often disintegrated. The loose head and the hooker were usually the first to come apart. Often, the Lions' tight head ended up pushing through the second row because the loose head had been drifted completely out of the scrum.

You can put pressure on your opposing prop in a number of ways, but all are dependent on having a good scrummaging unit around and behind you because a prop can never operate on his own. He must be supported by a good scrum and then he can transmit the efforts of the other forwards through to the opposition.

PRESSURE APPLIED BY THE PROP

(1) The easiest way to apply pressure is to scrummage at a level that your opponent finds uncomfortable. Most often, this is done by taking the scrum down to the point where your opponent cannot operate comfortably or effectively.

(2) As the scrummage is lowered, exert downward pressure with the right shoulder while lifting with the left. This moves your opponent in two directions, both of which he finds extremely uncomfortable.

(3) From the low position, thrust upwards and forwards as the ball comes into the scrum. This either unbalances or

shelves your man and diverts his efforts upwards rather than forwards.

(4) Putting your weight on the neck of your opponent rather than on his shoulders always puts extreme pressure on him.

PRESSURE APPLIED BY THE HOOKER

On his own ball, a hooker should exert downward pressure on his opposite number by dropping his right shoulder into his opponent's neck or alternatively using the same shoulder in a similar way to push his man further away from the ball. The closer the hooker and the loose head are on their own ball, the more difficult it is for the opposing tight-head to exert pressure on one or the other because both should be sharing the load.

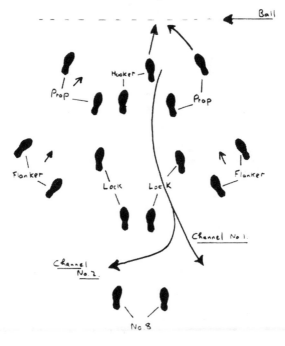

Scrummage foot positions for ball against the head.
Again the hooker is turned so that he can put downward pressure on his opponent with his right shoulder. The hooker then blocks the ball with his right foot and the tight head prop hooks it by following the ball in with a sweep of his right leg.

On the opposition's ball, and going for the eight-man shove, a hooker should exert as much downward pressure as possible on his opposite number to make it difficult for him to strike for the ball. If enough pressure is exerted, striking becomes impossible, and your own scrummage can win the ball simply by pushing over it.

In our pre-tour training at Eastbourne, the Lions concentrated very much on scrummaging because this was the one area of forward play where we were certain to be superior to the All Blacks. We concentrated on going down together as an eight and being settled immediately to eliminate any swinging of the scrum. This paid off handsomely. We repeatedly had really long and solid sessions of scrummage practice because we found that even on tour, it was surprising how quickly the co-ordination and the timing could be lost.

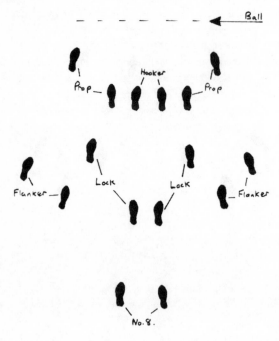

Scrummage foot positions for an eight-man shove.
The feet are pulled back and the pressure is directed downwards so that the opposing hooker either has difficulty in striking for the ball or cannot strike at all, in which case the loose head prop blocks the ball. This allows time for the push-over.

During the tour, the Lions scrummaged as low as possible to prevent the bigger New Zealand props following the ball in with their feet. This also offset the advantage in weight which the New Zealanders nearly always had. Instead of pulling their feet back as they should have done, the majority of New Zealand props stayed with their feet up. This meant that as soon as pressure was applied they buckled or were lifted or they had to twist to compensate for their bad position. As soon as this happened the scrum either collapsed or had to retreat as the second row and back row had nothing on which to bind and push. The foundation of a good scrummage did not exist. This put them at a tremendous disadvantage because even though they had an advantage in weight, they had nothing through which to transmit their power.

I would like to ask how many people have actually tried to coach a prop; who have actually said to a young prop, "You are not putting your feet in the right position" or asked a young hooker, "How do you put your opponent under pressure? What attitude, or in other words body position, do you adopt on your own ball as against the attitude you adopt against the head?"

The foot positions are the base on which we work. I feel that we have not looked closely enough at the foot positions of props and second rows and at the body positions of these men and the consequent application of power.

Many youngsters are working in the dark. They are having to get their knowledge from talking to someone who has just given them a hard time in the scrum to find out what mistakes they are making. As many of the old stagers realise that these are the people coming up, they try to help but it is very difficult to put into words what in many cases is an instinctive thing. There is a great feel to this position of propping in that you must be able to overcome a man who is stronger than you are by offsetting his strength with superior technique. Many people have a great advantage in weight so you must be able to put this to work for you instead of against you.

It is not enough to put a strong boy in to prop and let him find his way. So I would ask you to look at these positions as far as possible to help the players in them.

For much of the time in New Zealand the hookers used the left or near foot to strike on their own ball. As a result it was impossible to get near their ball so we concentrated on eight man pushing. This is done by lowering the scrum to put extra downward and forward pressure on the opposing front row and therefore limiting the space in which the hooker had to work and possibly of stopping him striking altogether by putting so much pressure on him that he could not lift his feet.

It goes without saying that in all eight-man pushes the hooker must pull his feet well back and push as hard as he can. It is dangerous to attempt to strike because the lowering of the front row would greatly increase the risk of collapsing the scrum if he did so. Eight-man pushes are more difficult in mud. It was in the mud for instance, in the second Test that we found difficulty in overcoming the All Blacks' advantage in weight because in mud it is impossible to pull the feet right back and scrummage really low. Also, with the give in the ground the shove often came too late and in those circumstances, real weight advantage is very difficult to overcome.

THE WORK OF THE FRONT ROW IN THE LINEOUT

Basically, the job of the front row in the lineout is to make contact with the opposition. The props' initial job is to protect their own jumper or to break through on opposing possession. The hooker at the front acts as a stopper on his own side's ball and as a pincer on the opposition's possession going round the front like a wing forward. The work of the front row in the line-out in New Zealand was strictly illegal. Making contact was done by stepping forward and into the opposition. The main objective was to prevent the opposing jumper from jumping and, at the same time, to stop your opponent doing the same thing to your own jumpers. In other words, your job was just to hold down as much as you could. Without this compression we would have been brushed aside so compression became the order of the day since possession depended on it.

The compression was achieved by all the forwards, except numbers one and eight, moving towards the ball wherever it was thrown. By doing this, you plug any gaps that may appear as you go forward. This stops the opposition breaking through on your own scrum-half, and by physically engaging the opposition, it enables you to support, protect and sometimes even to hide your own jumper.

From the lineout, props are generally used in supporting roles such as peels from the front and back. Their ball handling skill should be as good as the other members of the team. There is no reason why a big man and a strong man should not be able to handle as well as any three-quarter. The French can. Why can't we? Purely because we have labelled the prop as a donkey. He just grafts happily and sees the ball every two seasons.

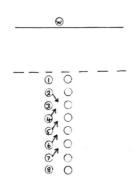

Ball thrown to number 3.

Hooker and number 8 float and position themselves as in Example 1. Number 2 moves backwards and inwards. Numbers 4, 5, 6 and 7 move forwards and inwards.

This movement towards the ball engages the opposition long enough for the scrum-half to make his pass. The tighter the lineout is to start with, the easier and more effective is the compression.

Ball thrown to number 5.

The hooker and the number 8 float at the front and the back to mop up, or by simply standing in a prudent position, to make it difficult for the opposition to get round them. As the ball is thrown, number 2, 3 and 4 move backwards and inwards and numbers 6 and 7 forwards and inwards. The role of number 6 is crucial.

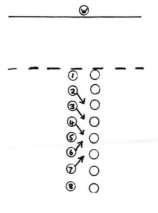

The work of the prop in the loose

As far as this is concerned, I believe that New Zealand have conned us for the best part of a century. They do exactly the same as we do in the rucks. If you are winning the ball, they lie on it. The only difference is that if you lie on it, they kick you. We found that they were exceptionally good ruck and maul players partly because at times they looked as if they would rather create a ruck than score a try. Their technique is much the same as ours, but they do it a little more quickly because generally they are faster round the field. Consequently, they arrive in greater numbers. It is this speed around the field which will make them a formidable force next season.

From the set piece, the tight five run on to a ruck founded generally by the back row. The last two or three men to arrive are generally the front row and they must arrive thinking about what they are doing. They don't just bash into it in the hope that the ball will pop out of it magically from within. They must size up the situation as they run across. They must be deciding long before they reach the ruck whether to join it or whether to fringe as a wing forward. It is not always to the benefit of the team that everybody goes into the ruck. Somebody must act as a fringer and at times it must be a prop forward or a hooker.

In all aspects of loose play props must be as alert as any member of the team. They must also run round the field thinking. Because in the modern game it is as likely that front row forward or second row forward will find himself in an open situation involving a running attack. When we look at the skill factors involved in running, catching and handling a ball there aren't very many that are very difficult. Basically - eye on the ball, hands out ready to catch or deliver the ball to a member of the same team.

I would like to give you some food for thought just as a finish. The demands on the modern player are great, but I think that we should be demanding more in the skill region from the front five. Most can scrummage well and can ruck and block and do their other jobs. But it is only the fringe skills, i.e. running and handling of the ball, in which most are weak. So let's put the

"They had the alternative of taking their feet back and lowering the scrum and not following the ball in, or being lifted. Most of them chose to be lifted." Ian McLauchlan, the Lions' tight head, fires Goddard, the Marlborough and Nelson Bays tight-head prop, through the top of the scrum at Blenheim. Flanker Derek Quinnell is obviously enjoying it, too.

Again, Derek Quinnell is an interested spectator. He has caused such havoc with his "compression" in the third Test at Wellington, that in desperation the All Blacks have split their lineout to isolate him. Gordon Brown, who is wrapped under Brian Lochore's shoulder lock, has deflected the ball to scrum-half Gareth Edwards. Ian McLauchlan (headband left) and Mervyn Davies (headband right) are still busily compressing. So is John Taylor on the far right, but he is literally so immersed in his task that he has almost buried himself in Ian Kirkpatrick.

demands on them that they are as good at handling and running with the ball as any other member of the team.

Q. How do you personally place your feet when you are scrummaging at loose head?

A. On most occasions, when it is our ball, I prop with my feet apart so that the hooker can come across and sit in front of my right thigh. This brings him as far across the tunnel as possible. On our ball, I do not try to attack. I regard myself as a holder of position. I try to bear the weight of the opposition and to provide my hooker with the stability and the space he needs. I push inwards with my outside foot and hold with my right foot, which I try to keep well clear so that there is a tunnel through which the ball can pass after it has been hooked. You should never attempt to twist either your feet or your body. Power comes from a straight line.

Q. Where does the lock put his head?

A. When we started to use this method in the Scotland pack, in which I stand more or less behind the hooker, there was a good question from Gordon Brown when he asked where he should put his head. I must confess that I still don't know where he puts it, but it gets there!

Q. Carwyn James has said that the opposing hooker was "scraping" in the Lions' game against King Country. What is scraping?

A. It is when a hooker flashes or rakes for the ball before it comes in. It is an attempt to anticipate the feed and it is foot-up but sometimes referees allow it, arguing that they are playing advantage. However, it does make it difficult for the scrum-half to put the ball into the scrum. On the occasion you mention, the Lions scrum-half was "Chico" Hopkins and the referee, Pat Murphy, kept saying, "Come on. Get the ball in! Get the ball in!"

Q. How did you manage to cope with a prop as heavy as "Jazz" Muller?

A. This is something I have been asked fairly frequently, as to how this chap Muller managed to stay in the game for so long! At the time we were in New Zealand, Muller was approximately four stones heavier than me and about five inches taller. He was a typical example of the prop who is somewhere over 18½ stones. He was one who came up, planted his feet and set himself almost exactly the same way each time. His feet were in the same position and he did practically the same thing in every scrum. He had a very big weight advantage, and according to the newspapers in New Zealand, he was so much stronger than I was that it was unbelievable.

However, as I have said, he was fairly predictable, so by a series of tricks of the trade, I was able largely to offset his advantage in weight as the game wore on. The early scrums were usually the most difficult. After those, I was usually able to take him into a position where he had to bend to get down to my level and this made him slightly uncomfortable. It also put pressure on his neck because he did not take his feet that bit further back and straighten his back and use his legs or alternatively weigh down on me and force me to hold his weight for a long period. Obviously, this would have been difficult for me.

For instance, one of the things I did was to keep him busy worrying about the arm binding. He wanted the outside bind, of course, which is the legal bind and occasionally I would just hold my arm away and force him to go inside and he would then be so busy trying to get this outside bind that by the time he had got it, the ball was in and away and I had had a wee rest because he was standing off.

I tried to vary the tactics in that respect, but as far as the body position went, I tried to stay with him, stay close to him. I did not allow him to get in and over the top of me. He wanted - or at any rate, I think this was what he wanted; I don't know whether he knew what he wanted himself - to stand up, more or less to stand off me and then come on me heavily. I stopped him doing this by taking him down and bending him and in this way offsetting his weight advantage. Also, by taking him down, this nullified his abilty to follow the ball in with his outside foot which he wanted to do all the time.

Outside the tests, many of the props we met in the provincial matches were very tall. They were around 6 ft 3 in.

Those boys were fairly easy to cope with because very few of them wanted to take their feet back. They wanted to bring their feet up so that they could follow the ball in and by taking them down that bit lower and putting the pressure on the upper part of their body, they were forced to bend. They then had the alternative of taking their feet back and lowering the scrum and not following the ball in, or of being lifted. Most of them chose to be lifted!

Q. *How did you personally scrummage on your own ball, and what did the pack do as a whole when it was pushed back?*

A. On our own ball, I scrummage slightly differently in that I try to act just a supporter for the hooker and to maintain a space at the mouth of the tunnel. In New Zealand, we used to do this a lot and the locks had their feet back to support this holding process.

If we were ever pushed back, the most important thing as far as we were concerned was to move back as a unit and not disintegrate. I think this was one of the main differences between us and New Zealand provincial packs. When they started to move back, they disintegrated because of their loose binding. They had no solid foundation because their front rows were so loose.

New Zealand hookers tended to strike with the near foot which meant that they got quick ball so if we intended to do an eight-man shove, the push had to go on really early so that they did not get the ball clear even though we were pushing them.

I got the impression that they had not thought very much about what to do about this scrummage drive except to get the ball into the scrum as quickly as possible and to get it out as quickly as possible.

Q. *Does it not block the channel if the locks scrummage with their outside feet up, and does it not hamper their channelling of the ball?*

A. I do not believe that it is the job of the second row to channel the ball. On your own ball, when the loose head adopts the holding position I have talked about and the hooker is striking for the ball, you have already reduced your pushing numbers to six and a half. If you then have your second row detailed to channel the ball, you further reduce the number of men pushing and you also reduce the strength of your most powerful contributors. We detailed the channelling to be done by the flanker or we brought the number eight over between the wing-forward and the left-hand lock occasionally. If the lock has his outside foot up, there is a natural channel if the hooker is striking right-footed because he sweeps the ball across.

Q. *What could Muller have done to make life more uncomfortable for you?*

A. He could have adjusted his feet in such a way so that he came down to my level, keeping a straight back, taking his legs back and being content not to strike for the ball and just bring this great weight to bear on either my neck or my shoulders. You can't support 18½ stone continuously for 80 minutes if a prop as heavy as that is continuously working on you.

He didn't try any of these things; in fact he concentrated more on trying to pull down with the arm. This did not work. He also tried turning in on the hooker which I don't think is a very good idea. Props should not try to work on their own. He was trying to do just that. This made my job much easier. As far as I was concerned, the lower the scrum was the better, and this suited John Pullin as well.

I think that the All Blacks' hooker was also a bit at fault because he never contented himself with putting pressure on Pullin probably because he knew that Pullin was so much stronger physically than he was. Norton kept trying to strike for the ball, instead of going for an eight man push.

(ADDITIONAL ANSWER BY RAY McLOUGHLIN)

This business about Muller being so much stronger than everybody else was an illusion. I don't think that he was that much stronger than Ian. There was a large quantity of non-productive weight in that 18½ stones. But he was no weakling, just the same.

I think that there were some things that he could have done to make things easier for himself, but I really could not be sure because it is not easy to see from a distance just what is happening in there.

First of all, I think that too many hookers want their props wrapped right in under them. One of the things that happens to a tight head in that situation is that he is held away from his opposing loose head prop. A loose head like Ian who is low and very strong can get underneath the tight head and can keep him turned inwards. Now the way to get that is to tell the hooker to go to hell, to bind loosely, to go outside as you go down and to wrap the loose head in under you. If the loose head gets in too quickly - as can happen when you are playing against Ian - the thing to do is to break away from the hooker and go out and go down quickly and then let the loose head get in when he wants and how he wants but you stay down there and leave your shoulder. The effect of that is this. The loose head may not be able to get his body and his back and his outside shoulder underneath the tight head and he needs to do that if he is going to get underneath him and lift him. He may only be able to get his neck in there, and once the other guy is down, it is very difficult to get under him.

So the speed with which you get down is important, so much so that if a tight head decides to do that, there is not much which you as a loose head can do unless he is very tall except dummy him, stand up and beat him to it when you go down again.

Q. *If you had one prop of 5 ft 9 in. and one of 6 ft 2 in. and other things like technique were roughly equal, which side of the scrum would you play them?*

A. Ian McLauchlan. I would play the short man on the loose head because it is easier for a small man to lift than a tall man. Again, if a tall man is playing at tight head, he can keep his feet reasonably far back and still have the length of leg to follow the ball in and strike against the head.

LOCK FORWARD PLAY

By *Geoff Evans*
(London Welsh and Wales)

For the purposes of this discussion I will split the functions of a lock into three parts:

(1) the lineout, (2) the scrum, (3) the loose.

But I want to emphasise that they must not be looked at as separate and distinct parts but rather as part of a whole.

LINEOUT PLAY

The object of this conference is to relate the specific aspects of play to what the Lions did, or were required to do, in New Zealand, and the first thing to say about what the Lions did in the lineout in New Zealand is that most of it was illegal. This was mainly due to the fact that when you are in Rome, you do as the Romans do, otherwise you get eaten by the bloody Lions!

From what I can make out, most of our players on previous Lions tours to New Zealand played reasonably within the limits of the laws. As a result, they won no ball. They were pushed and pulled and barged about and generally frustrated. Colin Meads put this rather well in Wanganui when he said that on previous Lions' tours, he had the impression that the British believed in fairy tales. So we decided to come down to reality.

To do this, we had to accomplish three things. The first was to build a solid wall to protect the scrum-half from the likes of "Jazz" Muller. We did this fairly well, although there were occasions when our half-backs received some hefty blows. Fortunately, there was some compensation for them, because they usually resulted in three points from a kick by Barry John.

Having built this wall, the next step was to develop the technique of compressing the lineout. Basically, the idea of this is to exert as much pressure as possible from as many different directions as possible to wherever the ball is thrown in the line-out. There has to be unanimous action near the ball. If only one player attempts to provide this compression, he is invariably penalised. The aim of this compression is to give your jumper some freedom of action so that he can get off the ground and has some chance of catching or palming the ball back. If we forgot to compress - and sometimes concentration did lapse - no one got off the ground and the ball went to the longest arm.

Side by side with this compression, we used the "step" theory. Again this emanated from New Zealand, from the 1967 All Blacks, though it had been used by New Zealand sides for many years before that. Anyway, we thought that we would try to beat them at their own game.

It is only in the last couple of seasons that this particular technique has been much in evidence in this country. Essentially, the "step" involves the whole eight forwards in the line taking one step towards the opposition. It can be argued that if there is a space between two lines of forwards, the ball has to be thrown in the middle, then obviously the forwards have to go in after it to win the ball. It can also be argued that all the forwards are entitled to see themselves as ball winners, and so all are entitled to go for it, particularly as any number of factors can affect the throw and much of the possession which comes out of a lineout is largely a matter of chance. The essence of the "step" theory is unanimity. All the forwards must do it in concert. It is no good just one or two forwards doing it.

In the match between Wales and Scotland this year, it was decided beforehand that at the first lineout on or near the Scottish 25, all the Welsh forwards would take this step and knock the Scottish forwards towards their own line in the hope that Wales would win the ball. What happened was that I remembered to do it and nobody else did and I was penalised.

However, the basic idea of the step is a good one, because if the ball is not won cleanly after it has been thrown in, the probability is that it will bobble about and come down on your side because you have moved underneath the line of the throw.

By a combination of compressing the lineout at the point of the throw and taking this step towards the opposition, the Lions were able to win much more of the ball than most of their predecessors to tour New Zealand. The Lions still did not win a fantastic amount of lineout ball, particularly in the tests, but at least what we did achieve was a considerable improvement.

We can argue about the morality of using illegal tactics to win the ball but I have simply stated what we did. However, I do think that this is an opportune moment to discuss lineout laws in general.

There are so many laws relating to this part of play that a referee would need four pairs of eyes to watch for them all. Therefore, most of the infringements which are committed in every lineout in every game must of necessity go undetected. In this instance, crime most certainly does pay.

Therefore, why not take steps to legalise some of these crimes? After all, the aim of the lineout is presumably to ensure that the ball is won cleanly by one side or the other, so it could be argued that means which assist in this aim should be allowed.

I would like to suggest three possibilities. The first concerns the magic word of: LIFTING.

Most clubs and countries use this technique, and those that don't use it, don't win the ball. Obviously some sides and some players are more adept at this than others and those sides and players usually win a lot of ball.

Now I see no reason why lifting should not be legalised, because it does produce good clean ball and that is what the game wants. If it was legalised, it would allow referees to concentrate on other illegalities instead of spending their time nipping from the front to the back and from side to side looking for lifting which they will never see if the players concerned in the lifting process have any degree of nous. Lifting is illegal at the moment, but I see no reason why it should not be made a part of the game.

Reintroduction of blocking

At the moment, all sorts of ploys are used to prevent a jumper getting off the ground – pushing him out of the lineout, pulling his jersey or his shorts, standing on his feet. It is possible to interfere in other ways in the course of the jump, but in most cases the offenders are the props on the opposing sides.

If blocking were to be reintroduced, the prop forwards could drive in on their opposite numbers and could involve themselves happily in their own private little battles, while allowing the respective jumpers more chance of a clean jump.

It could be argued that the law concerning the gap down the middle of the lineout should make interference impossible. This it patently does not do, so to my mind it is a bad law. Any law which does not work is a bad law.

If blocking was re-introduced, then the possibility of setting up good attacks behind the scrum would increase.

DOUBLE BANKING

This was abandoned after an experimental period which many people feel was too short to be of value. In my opinion, it was abandoned because it gave the scrum-half too much time to decide what to do with the ball and in most cases he decided to kick it.

Since that time, though, touch-kicking has been restricted and I would argue that if double-banking was used properly nowadays, it would give the half-backs more time to set up their backs in attacks. It would also introduce some badly needed variations in attacking ploys from a lineout by the forwards. At the present time, the only attacks made by forwards from the lineout are peels or rolls, whatever you prefer to call them, round the back and much less frequently, peels round the front.

In the early days, when the French instigated this tactic, they were very successful indeed. Nowadays, though, they are becoming less and less successful because the defending team knows reasonably well how to combat it.

This is not always the case. I remember a game at the end of last season, for instance, when Sandy Carmichael took a peel and ran straight at an illustrious outside-half who has just retired! That outside-half side-stepped him neatly and Carmichael scored. In most cases, though, the operation of the peel is not altogether successful. The forwards run too far across, they don't breach the defence as they should so that in most cases now, the defence is in control.

If double banking was brought back, I think that another direction of attack could be developed with more running from the big forwards from the double-banked set-piece. After all, we donkeys do like a run now and then!

If I may add a footnote to my remarks about the lineout, I should make a reference to throwing in. This is the starting point of the lineout and it is one of the most important aspects. No matter if you have the best lineout forwards in the world, everything comes to nothing if the throw is not accurate. This was one of the best features of the Lions' lineout play. Their throwing was good. A considerable amount of practice was devoted to it on tour and all our wingers did well. Of course, the wingers do not necessarily have to do the throwing in. It can be the hooker, but whoever it is, let him go away and practice and practice so that he can put the ball exactly where he wants to.

SCRUMMAGING

This was the cornerstone of the success of the Lions. I must say at the outset that good scrummaging depends on good props and the Lions were indeed fortunate that they had five excellent props.

The lock's job in the scrummage is less arduous than that of the props because he has a straightforward role to play. He must push hard and he must make sure that his shove is being transmitted in the right direction. I pack on the right of the scrum, and there is nothing I hate more than packing behind a so-called destructive tight head prop, because all these men do is bore in. If you try to push on them, all you succeed in doing is to push their backside further and further out. Consequently, you transmit very little push. If the prop pushes straight, it is much easier to get going in a forward direction. Therefore, I feel strongly that it is the job of a tight forward to push in a straight line and not at an angle.

BINDING

I think that the best way to bind is on the inside leg of the prop. From the simple principles of mechanics, it is obviously easier to hold the prop in and bind tight with the arm held more or less in front of the chest than it is to hold the prop in by binding round his backside. It is the same principle as Indian wrestling. The closer to your body that your arm is, the more power it has. Also, by binding round the rump of your prop, you interfere with the scrummaging of the flanker, and these days, the best flankers DO scrummage.

COMMUNICATION BETWEEN BACKS AND FORWARDS

This is essential, because the forwards can save valuable seconds by knowing in advance in which direction they have to run. This alone can make all the difference between a decisive piece of second phase possession and a killed ball. The communication must come from the scrum-half. He knows what move the backs are going to do and he must tell his forwards, by means of a code signal.

Delme Thomas, blocked by Gordon Brown (No. 4), "Stack" Stevens (head burrowing) and John Taylor (with beard), wins the ball against Southland.

LOOSE PLAY

All forwards must have the ability to run and think. Some people see tight forwards simply as ball-getters. That is not enough. The presence of the tight forwards at a point of breakdown is usually decisive, so the essential is to get there. Rucking and mauling technique is useless if the forward physically cannot get to the point of breakdown or to a position in which he can provide support, so he must push himself to the utmost to do so. A gentle amble is not enough.

Q. *Were there any special problems attached to playing against Colin Meads and Peter Whiting in the lineout? And how were the pairings of the locks arrived at?*

A. I did not play against Meads, but I did play against Whiting and a number of other jumpers in New Zealand, and as has been said already, the basic way to tackle these people is not to do so as an individual but as part of an organisation. The formula had been worked out very thoroughly by the time I arrived in New Zealand as a replacement and my job as a jumper was made much easier by the support which was provided by all the other forwards. They all helped me into a position where I could get the ball.

There was still a lot to be done because the opposition fellow was obviously just not going to stand there, and to quote a famous remark, in many instances it was a case of getting your retaliation in first. You knew what was coming and if you didn't do something about it at the very beginning you quickly found yourself in an impossible situation. It did not matter what pack of forwards you were up against in New Zealand, unless you showed and showed very quickly that you did not give a damn about them or their reputations then they would think of you as a fairy. Once they had gained this psychological advantage over you, they could grind you. The important thing was not to yield to this psychological pressure and to exert psychological pressure of your own with whatever part of your anatomy you cared to use before he did it to you. This exchange of courtesies was essential before you could even begin to play!

As far as working with another lock is concerned, I believe in the current fashion of using complementary jumpers, because the techniques of jumping at two or three are completely different from those needed further back in the lineout. The chap who jumps at the front does not usually have the opportunity or the time to jump very high. Willie John McBride and myself operated there, with Gordon Brown and Delme Thomas jumping at numbers four and five.

At the front, you can take a hard, low ball or you can take a lob. As long as your opponent is standing level with you, your knowledge of the type of throw and its target will give you just enough time to beat him. If he moves forward to two, then you signal your wing to lob the ball over him. If he then comes back again, you revert to the hard, low ball.

I found that in New Zealand, quite a lot of provincial jumpers liked the hard, low ball at the front, so when it became obvious that they were going to throw a short ball, I would occasionally go up to number one.

Now you would think that they would then have had the intelligence to lob the ball over my head to number three. But no. Not a bit of it.

I remember in the Hawke's Bay game, for example, that this chap did not alter his throw at all, and kept on hurling it at me like a bullet about six feet off the ground. Straight at me at number one! I just caught it and flicked it straight back. This showed a certain lack of thought on their part, I felt!

So I think that it is very important to choose complementary locks, because the techniques are so different. The specialist short line ball-getter - I ought not to use the word jumper, especially in relation to New Zealand - and the specialist ball-getter at number five have to approach their jobs in entirely different ways.

Q. Is the return of the two-handed jumper important?

A. Jumping at number two or three in the lineout, it is possible to catch the ball. With the situation as it is at number five, however, the jumper has very little chance of going up and catching the ball two-handed. There is too much interference.

Scrummaging with the locks binding on the inside leg of their props. This is a powerful arm position.

...And it allows the flanker to adopt an equally powerful position like the one John Taylor has adopted here. It is comfortable, his body position is good and he is transmitting his shove in a way which is giving his prop maximum assistance.

Geoff Evans, scrummaging at right lock in the London Welsh pack, adopts the bind outside his prop's hips. This is the bind commonly used in New Zealand but has been rejected in Britain because of its slackness and because it hampers the scrummaging of the flanker.

Apart from its inherent weakness, the outside bind forces the flanker either to waste his energies and positively hamper his prop by pushing in the back of the prop's knee…

Or the flanker slides up on to the rump of the prop and forces his lock to slide his bind round the prop's waist and to lose his own scrummaging position completely.

RAY WiLLiAMS (COACHiNG ORGANiSER, WELSH RUGBY UNION)

I was interested to hear Geoff talking about the importance of dominating your opponent psychologically. It reminded me of that lovely story about Colin Meads in the game against Scotland at Murrayfield in 1967.

Now Meads was opposed by a youngster called Erle Mitchell, who was winning his first cap for Scotland, and legend has it that at some convenient lineout early in the game when there was a bit of a wait while they fetched the ball, Meads told Mitchell in some detail just what he was going to do to him for the rest of the match. Apparently, it was quite a speech. Well, Mitchell told his team-mates about this afterwards and they listened goggle-eyed as he went into all the details. When he had finished, one of them said to Mitchell, "And what did you say to him, Erle?"

Mitchell replied, "I told him to bugger off. But I have to admit, I didna say it in a very loud voice!"

As far as the two-handed catch is concerned, it is almost impossible to achieve this at number five. If we want the return of the two-handed catch, and obviously it makes for tidier possession, then we will have to change the lineout laws pretty drastically. The

International Board have this subject on their agenda, and we in the Welsh Rugby Union are going to try some experiments on our selected courses at Aberystwyth. One of the big problems of changing the law is that too often, one does not know if the change will work. We hope to provide some answers in advance.

LOOSE FORWARD PLAY

By *John Taylor*
(London Welsh and Wales)

There have been many controversies in recent years revolving around back row play and the sort of person who should play in the back row. Most of these have become somewhat more heated since we have had changes in the laws in recent years which generally have given half-backs more room to move with the idea hopefully, of creating more open rugby. I refer, of course, to the law relating to the time at which a wing-forward is allowed to detach himself from the scrum and the law which requires that nobody except the scrum-half be within ten yards of the lineout.

Before these changes in the laws, I think that the back row forward was undoubtedly neither a proper forward nor a proper back. He was something of a trained hunter. He was there to pursue and to attempt to destroy his half-back quarry throughout the game. His tackling ability was his greatest asset and I can remember quite a few and there are still some of them playing at this time who were a dead loss in any other phase of the game. Geoff Evans has talked about the second-row and Ian McLauchlan has talked about front row forwards who never think about handling and who ought to. Well, I think that the same is probably true of back row forwards to an extent.

Now with these changes in the law, the wing forward and the number eight have become definitely complete and wholehearted forwards. The wing forward's job has moved towards what used to be the prerogative of the number eight before the laws were changed, but I think we must realise that we are still in a transitional stage as far as this goes and that there are quite a few players still around who are seeing out the end of their careers -

successfully in quite a number of cases. I don't want to mention names but I am sure you can think of a few of them and they are doing quite well playing the old sort of game.

Two of the most advertised controversies have been about the question of playing open and blind side wing forwards and one about which I am a little sensitive, of course - the question of size. If Bill McLaren says once more, "There's big Mervyn Davies at No. 7 and wee John Taylor behind him," I'll probably stuff him! Still, I will admit McLaren is great for British Rugby.

I hope to make as the main point of my paper that most of what is said about these particular controversies is said in such dogmatic terms that it rarely looks at the whole situation in its full context. We tend to look perhaps at the most successful side at the moment and try to imitate them even if we are playing a completely different brand of football.

I personally believe that British, New Zealand, South African and French styles of play are all evolving somewhat differently and that therefore, the back rows are also evolving differently, and that one must look at conditions in the countries and the style of games that those countries are trying to play before one starts to look at what one expects from a back row forward. In recent years New Zealand back row forwards have probably been the tightest because their whole game has been dominated completely by their forwards. Their pattern of play has been very simple. Once the ball has been won and gone into the back division the aim usually - particularly when they had Ian MacRae playing at second five eighth - was to set up a ruck which the forwards could pile into.

They used very big back row forwards and they tended to set up the ruck fairly close to where the set piece had taken place. It was very interesting for me to go back to New Zealand with the Lions this time in a successful side, and for the first time to win enough ball and to be playing in a situation where we could turn some of the tables on the All Blacks, and see somebody like Ian Kirkpatrick in a completely different light. I don't think that I am doing him an injustice to say that he is not at all the same player when he is going backwards as he is when he is going forwards. This is partly because of what he has been used to. I rate him as perhaps the greatest attacking wing forward in the world at the moment, especially in British and New Zealand conditions. In these circumstances he excels, but once you start asking him to tackle forwards who are coming at him and backs who are coming at him, he is not quite the same player.

The South African back row forwards are very adept at picking up a loose ball and at mauling, because in South Africa grounds are generally hard and most of the tight-loose phase of the game tends to be mauls rather than rucks because the ball pops up from those hard grounds, and when I was there in 1968 the South African forwards were very, very good at doing it. They are probably better than anyone else in the world.

In this country, I think that we have our strengths too. We are a very maligned lot, but one of the things we are probably better at than any other wing forwards in the world is tackling. The reason for this is probably that when we have been playing against the other major rugby countries we have won less ball and so we have bloody well had to tackle. I think it is not conceited to say that British back row forwards - especially at tackling backs - are probably the best in the world.

Now that a British style of play is evolving where we are moving the ball to the backs we are also becoming quite good at supporting directly play which is a long way from a set piece. We are very good at taking a ball directly from a back's hands and at getting into the position to be able to do this.

I intend to go into the question of open and blind side at greater length at a later stage, but if I might digress just a little on the size factor it will get it out of my system and then we can all forget it. Obviously, a good big one will beat a good little one providing that he can do all that the little one can do, but very often he can't. This is where we have to think in terms of priorities.

If a pack is weak in size and weight, then obviously a small back row is not going to help that aspect of its play at all, and therefore this must become a priority. If a side is playing a ten-man game then again one must evaluate what the back row are going to be doing and size again could be a very important factor.

The opposites might well apply as well. It is no use having a big heavy man who can be very effective in a situation close to a set piece if he cannot get to the situation where you are trying to work an overlap to put a winger away.

What I do object to is someone saying that you are too small and then advocating the selection of somebody who is half an inch taller and three pounds heavier. What there is no answer to is the Welsh flanker who came up to me last season and said, "Look. I am two stone heavier than you. I'm four inches taller. I can run faster. My 'ands are better and you're a fairy. Why aren't I playing for Wales?"

I had to say I just don't know.

Let's look a little closer at the specific function of the back row. Although I think that it is dogmatic to talk about units the back row is involved in two units - one with the half-backs who share the link job in the team, and the other unit obviously is being part of the pattern. Again I must emphasise that although the back row have to do this link job with their half backs, wing-forwards and number eights must never lose sight of the fact that they are first and foremost forwards. They are responsible mainly for the continuity phase of play and this obviously covers lots of things - supporting the man with the ball, winning the ball from rucks and mauls and generally linking between the forwards and backs. I think it is important to remember that Rugby Union gains it character and its main difference from Rugby League in its continuity. It is interesting to me to see that Rugby League has now developed itself to such an extent as a so-called spectator sport that it is all stop go, stop go, stop go and you get a one against one situation all the time. In fact, it has worked itself to a standstill and as a spectator sport it has declined in consequence. Our game is doing the opposite. We are becoming more competent in this country at this continuity of winning ball from the rucks, of getting ball from situations other than set pieces and keeping the game going.

The whole aim of attack - apart from the individual who is brilliant enough to run through somebody - is to create a situation where you outnumber your opponents. The overlap is obviously the simplest method of doing this and one of the most effective, but the ruck is an equally important way of achieving the same end. It will often tie up defenders so that having won the ball from the ruck, a change of direction will find an uncovered area and the possibility of a score. It certainly upsets the one to one situation which exists from a set piece and it is an area where the back row can be and usually are the deciding factor.

From a set situation the wing forward should be the first to arrive at a break down or a check and it is obviously his job to secure the ball somehow. Again, I don't think that it is any use being dogmatic. The way that the job is done depends on the size and strength and the sort of player you have. Obviously, there are some rules that we must lay down but I have seen so many different players using so many different but successful techniques that one of the things I don't intend to do is to say, "Do it this way," or, "Do it that way."

What I hope to be able to do is to persuade people to keep uppermost in their minds what they are trying to do. I think that there are lots of times when a player tears across the field, gets to the tackle, gets to the ruck situation, and thinks, "I've made it. Great. That's my job done. I'm here. Where's the rest of them?"

That is when his job starts. It seems a silly thing to say but we do fall down on that aspect of the game, particularly in this country.

As far as rucks and mauls go, obviously ball in the hand is more easily controlled than ball on the floor but equally obviously it is not always possible to get it there. What is important is the base the back row can form for the rest of the forwards.

We have been very poor in this country at staying on our feet and the New Zealand forwards have been very good at it. This has been one of the deciding factors between the two countries in the past decade.

Often a diligent but unthinking back row forward is responsible for this heap of bodies that we call a ruck in this country. It is more difficult for a small man to stay on his feet than a big man, and if we are going to play smaller back row forwards - and I think that this trend is probably general in this country because as I have mentioned before I don't really see all these big men who are supposed to come in and take my place; there just don't seem to be a lot of them around playing in the back row at this time, then staying on our feet is one thing we should really work on in our training in this country. If we have smaller men in the back row then we must make sure that they are really strong.

In set plays, the back row has to be especially flexible and yet there is probably more dogma about what should and should not be done in this phase of the game than any other. I have spent years trying to prove that flankers do actually push in the scrums - which Geoff Evans has now conceded - but having done this I then got into a situation where it became an obsession with me and when we went to New Zealand, I really had to start re-thinking my whole policy about pushing because of what happened in the second Test.

In this Test, the victory the New Zealanders had was largely due to the Lions' back row getting up from the scrum too late to contain the opposing back row and scrum-half. The All Blacks' penalty try came directly from Sid Going breaking on the blind side, my side, having got the ball at that stage while his pack was being moved backwards at a rate of knots with our back row and me in particular thinking what a good job we were doing in rollicking the All Black pack backwards.

It was a prime case to me of not thinking and thereafter Carwyn got hold of us and we played the thing very differently. Once the push has been initiated it is very hard to counter and if the ball has nevertheless been heeled by the opposition despite that push one must allow the possibility that however fast they are going back they will still manage to get the ball out of the back of their scrum. Therefore the flankers must still be ready to stop any break at that point. In the third Test in New Zealand we disobeyed all the progressive thinking as far as back row play goes. We went back to an open and blind side system. We went back to saying that Derek Quinnell will play blind side and will look after Sid Going who likes to break on that side, and John Taylor will harass in the open and get amongst the backs to stop them moving the ball.

Bob Burgess and Sid Going had been king-pins of the second Test victory by the All Blacks. We felt that if we cut them out we just had to win because even in the second Test, the signs had been there that this was only the department of the team and the game where they had an advantage over us.

Therefore, the job of the flanker will vary considerably relative to the dominance or lack of it in the scrums.

In the lineouts the flankers' job varies depending on where he stands. We have heard a lot about compression. It all applies to the back row. The only thing I do feel, if I may have another little dig at the lineout laws, is that at the end of the lineout compression is very, very difficult. Geoff Evans says that he has never known a referee to have four pairs of eyes. I constantly get blamed and I think every player who stands at number eight in the lineout gets blamed for allowing opposing players to come behind him.

One important point of the referees' job with the law as it stands ought to be to make sure that the side throwing in the ball controls the length of the lineout as the law requires. Unfortunately, with all the other things the referee has to do he cannot possibly do that and it is virtually impossible unless you are very illegal to stop an opponent coming round behind you. You have to resort to holding or barging or knocking the man out of the way.

The boys have already mentioned - and I will readily endorse - that particularly for a small man like me, New Zealand was a haven, a Godsend, as far as this went.

Mervyn Davies and I had a lovely battle at the back of the lineout with the All Blacks' loose forwards which I think we gradually won. They were very dominant at the beginning of the tour but by the end of the tour Mervyn was getting the ball fairly cleanly and there were a lot of threats as to what they were going to do with us. Very few of these threats came to anything.

I was left quite free by the referee to set about my business and to just clean out Kirkpatrick and Wyllie as best I could. It all came to a head in the fourth Test when I think they had been given orders on intimidation by their coach as the only way they were going to win it. In the first ten minutes Kirkpatrick who had been telling me for three months that, "The next time you do that, you are going to get stuffed," actually sent one at me. He missed me and hit Mervyn. I threw one and missed him and hit Wyllie which left Wyllie and me standing there glowering at each other while Mervyn and Kirkpatrick went away and sorted it out by themselves.

Geoff Evans talked about leaving the jumper free to jump and the one thing I would say on this is that I do not think that enough thought has been given to where the man actually doing the jumping at the back of the lineout should stand. In New Zealand we had the situation where we had one tall man and two men who were not so tall so Mervyn was the obvious lineout jumper.

In New Zealand if the jumper is going to be effective I think it is very important to have a man behind him as we did because New Zealand forwards constantly jostle to get behind the opposing jumper so that they can push him forward and leave themselves with a free jump.

In this country where the referees do not allow quite so much compression I think that there is probably a far bigger case in terms of freedom of the man to jump for allowing him to jump at number eight. Again, this brings us back to the main point that I am trying to make which is that we have to think relative to the game that we are about to play, to the opposition we are about to meet and to our side on that particular day.

Perhaps we have got to think out every game and change our tactics each time accordingly.

The other thing which I think we are especially bad at in this country is in our attack from the back row in set pieces. Perhaps again size or lack of it is the reason for this and this is one of the things that we have to put up with if we are going to choose back rows who are physically small. Perhaps it is a good reason for getting rid of back rows who are physically small. However, in a number of cases it is also because of a lack of liaison with the scrum-half.

The Lions' loose forwards had six basic set moves in attack. They did not feature as significantly and in the pattern of the team as they might have done because it was felt that the area of loose forward play was one of the strengths of the New Zealand team and that therefore it would be better to play away from that strength and towards a weakness. This policy was certainly justified by the success of the Lions' backs.

To me there are basically two sets of back row moves:

(1) The move that relies mainly on the power and strength of an individual.

(2) The move that involves a forward making an extra man who can make space for somebody else.

However, the loose forward moves which we held in reverse were:

(1) The right flanker breaks to the left of a scrum as the ball is heeled and takes a shielded pass from his scrum-half who takes out his opposite number. Code word: London Welsh.

This move is very effective if the flanker can link with the backs but the difficulty with it is to provide support from the other loose forwards.

(2) The number 8 breaks to the right of a scrum and takes a flat pass from the scrum-half. Code: a Welsh word, which I can't spell!

The biggest problem with this move is for the number 8 to achieve any momentum. If he is powerfully built and fast and has great strength in his legs, it can be a good move. The number 8 tries to thrust forward and looks inside for support, first from the left flanker rolling round the scrum and then from the right flanker.

(3) The number 8 picks up the ball from the back of the scrum and feeds the scrum-half breaking right.

This move was more successful because the scrum-half was able to work up a little more acceleration and with a half-back as strong as Gareth Edwards, he was able to achieve the impact of a flanker. Code: another Welsh word which I can't spell!

(4) The right flanker packs at number 8. The number 8 packs into the slot between the left flanker and the right flanker. The number 8 picks up and takes out the opposing scrum-half from the scrum going left.

This was a good move to support from the rest of the back row. Referees sometimes said that the number 8 was in front of the hindmost foot. This is arguable but in any case it is possible to get round it by properly controlling the heel.

(5) The same move as number (4) except with the loose forwards packed on the right of the scrum. The advantage of doing the move on that side was that the opposing scrum-half was not in the way. The problem is that without a flanker on the left of the scrum, it is much more difficult to channel the heel to the right place. Also, there is occasionally a danger of accidental offside.

(6) The Brian Lochore move. In this, the number 8 breaks right either before or as the ball goes into the scrum. He takes a pass from his scrum-half and turns his back to shield the direction of his pass. He can either dummy or pass to a back running on a scissors line going inside or he can either dummy or pass to a back or a loose forward going outside, or he can put together a combination of the two. He can even retain the ball and if he is not tackled by the opposing number 8, which is the basic defence to this move, he can turn and thrust for the line himself. This move is invariably used from a scrum in an attacking position.

Even allowing for the fact that the Lions' backs returned a quicker profit for us further away from the scrum, I don't think that we used the back row in attack as much as we should have done. Of course, physically we were not as strong as the All Blacks' loose forwards and therefore in moves which involve generating power from a static position, we were at a disadvantage. Obviously, 16 stones give you a better chance of making a dent. As far as the Lions were concerned, the most crucial factor in the success of loose forward moves was always timing.

I am sure that not enough thought is given to the selection of moves which suit the back row playing at that time. The Lochore move I have described was used so successfully by the All Blacks throughout the 1960s, that it became a classic example. It is a move which has been copied more than any other simply because it was done very well by a successful New Zealand team.

However, I think we must look at the strength of the players involved before committing ourselves to one move or another. The Lochore move is usually not successful in this country because we get the wrong person taking the ball and trying to use himself as a battering ram or the wrong person standing out of the scrum and distributing the ball from the Lochore type position. No thought is given to it. The attitude has been, "The All Blacks did that so it must be a good move. Let's go ahead and copy them."

It is usually not successful to have a small man as a battering ram unless he has worked up a lot of pace so that the first type of move I have described is generally out if you have small back row forwards. Similarly it is useless to try to work the sort of move that is going to put a very big, strong, slow loose forward into a gap that he is not going to be able to exploit. I am not going to go in to what sort of moves we should use because I hope to be playing for a couple more years and I think this is one of the secrets that one tries to keep to stay one ahead of the people that you are playing against. What I will say is that I am sure that we have not tapped the reservoir of loose forward moves that are possible. I do not think I have seen more than six different moves since I have been playing. I am sure there are 25.

The last point I would like to make on loose forward moves is that when we practice them I think that we tend to do so until they work in practice but not necessarily in a match situation. This was one of the things on tour that did not really apply because we were playing the sort of football that meant that we were exploiting such a weakness in the New Zealand backs generally that our principle aim nearly all the time was to move the ball away to the backs. Consequently, we did not use the loose forwards for attacking ploys very much. It is no reflection on Carwyn to say that we did not practise them because we were operating in a special set of circumstances. Still, I think we can learn from the soccer people who go on practising, practising, practising until a move stands up under pressure.

In rugby, especially if the captain happens to be a back, we too often see the situation in this country where a back row move is called which hasn't been practised enough and when it fails the whole thing is discarded because the captain is a bit dispirited, and the other side have gained 50 yards. The skipper curses the back row. I would suggest that this is probably a fault in the way we practice.

If we go on to look at defence, again I think that the changes in the laws have made a great difference to the job of the loose forwards. A great deal has been talked about the roles of the individuals. When I was learning the game at school the number eight corner flagged for the whole game and I can't see how he and the rest of the back row ever got into the game. However, at that stage I was playing centre so it did not affect me but all I can remember is those guys running along behind the backs and playing a double full-back game.

In a lot of people's minds the wing forward is still thought to be a failure if he doesn't nail his fly-half every time.

These are all absolutes that are obviously dangerous. I cannot see how a wing forward can touch a fly-half from a lineout or a scrum if that fly half's aim is simply to catch and to give the ball and yet this is still a point that is used as an evaluation of a wing forward. If the fly-half is going to try to break then certainly the flanker must be in a position to do something about it.

But again this is a plea for objective thinking rather than following blindly the old adages and traditions churned out by people who haven't really thought about the game.

Dr. Tom Kemp said when we started, "We are in a new era." That is very true so let's not allow people who are not really a part of that era, not so much in terms of age but in terms of getting geared into it, to keep pushing these old ideas at us.

Methods of defence depend on a variety of factors and again on what sort of players you have available, on what sort of players you have about you.

If as a flanker I am playing with Barry John outside me at fly-half, my attitude towards defence is completely different from what it is if I am playing with Bob Phillips, the London Welsh fly-half. Bob is a very strong tackler. Barry is the world's greatest exponent of fingertip tackling! He doesn't believe that it is a part of his job, though he has been known under pressure to deign to go down and touch somebody's boots. It depends who you're against as well. The New Zealand half-backs in recent years have been a good example of the comparisons one can make. Chris Laidlaw made his reputation as the man who brought the spin pass into fashion. He can set up his backs very quickly and is not renowned so much as a runner.

Sid Going, on the other hand, is exactly the opposite. He is very much like Gareth Edwards in his running though they use slightly different techniques, but as a flanker your first thought when you are playing against Sid is that he is going to be coming round the scrum.

The only thing I think you can do is to lay down priorities. Defence around the scrum is obviously the responsibility of the back row. The harassment of the half-backs and the prevention of breaks is also the responsibility of the back row. But one must make sure that it is in that order.

How does one defend against a fly-half? One tries to push him out, if you are playing with a non-tackling fly-half so that he crowds his backs. On the other hand, if I am playing with a tackling fly-half, we probably try to sandwich our opponent between us and stop him going either way. But again there is this need for evaluation.

I have mentioned the half-backs and obviously they are very important in defence, so I think this is a good moment to come back to the relations of the back row with the half-backs. There has to be a lot of understanding and cooperation and I think that this is more often lacking than it would appear. The loose forwards often feel that they are not trusted by their half-backs. I have certainly felt that at various stages. The half-backs might have been right, but psychologically it is not good to make the loose forwards feel that they are not trusted.

A lot of people ask the half-backs, who are the star boys, "What do you expect of your back row?" Very few people ask the opposite question and say to the back row, "What do you expect of your half-backs?" But I am going to answer that question in any case.

The first thing is that the back row wants to be trusted by the half-backs. We have heard this word "donkeys" bandied around. It was certainly bandied around in New Zealand and the forwards became very conscious of being donkeys, but then two of the most successful backs were John Bevan and John Williams and they were definitely donkeys so we felt a bit better about that!

We all got various donkey gradings as we went along. The King certainly wasn't a donkey, but John Dawes qualified for at least a couple of ears. Gerald Davies had a pedigree, Mike Gibson was a donkey at times because he tackled and the rest of the backs didn't like that. But having mentioned that, I think that this is the other thing that a back row forward certainly respects tremendously from half-backs. If you are playing with half-backs you get a great feeling of security if you know that they are strong in a position where skills are at a premium. It is a great boost to see a half-back clear up his own mistake or go down on the ball and not say, "Uh, uh! Something's gone wrong. Come on, donkeys! Down you go! That's your job, not mine. I'll have the ball again when it's all been cleared up."

Obviously we do feel a responsibility for that and we consider that it is our job but equally obviously there are times when somebody has to take responsibility other than the back row, and it is very nice when you are playing with half-backs who will take that responsibility.

Barry John has other qualities, like being able to walk on the water and fly...

It goes without saying that this is not the be-all and end-all. I would not advocate dropping Barry John even though he does not measure up to any of the things we have mentioned about defence. He has got other qualities like being able to walk on the water and fly!

I think that the England back row last season were probably very sad when Jan Webster was dropped. He is the epitome of the half-back who is strong in defence. He is almost a third wing forward in his tackling. This gives us food for thought again. After all the scrum-half is the only player who, since the change in the laws, is really able to get round the scrum and get after his opposing half-back. He can even go after the fly-half if he knows that the scrum-half is going to be feeding all the time. This is something which most scrum-halves have never even considered.

In attack, this strength factor also comes in. It is a great boost to play with Gareth Edwards or Sid Going because they have this strength and can become the major initiators of attack. Here again we must link back to attacking from the back row. Having Gareth there in the Welsh side means with his peculiar brand of strength which seems to fox so many people that he is the obvious man to initiate attacks from the back row. I wish that for just once he would look inside and see me screaming and yelling and running beside him instead of always looking outside for his ruler, the King!

In New Zealand it is the opposite, and I think it is a reflection on the players concerned that 99 times out of 100, Sid Going will always link inwards and join up with a forward rather than a back because this is the way that their rugby is geared.

I can sum up by re-iterating and emphasising the thing I started with. A loose forward's game must be flexible and he must approach each problem as it comes. Although it is a position which requires almost continuous motion, it requires also split second decisions. Whether or not to join a ruck? This is especially important when the second ruck is forming. You get accused of being a sea-gull and hanging out and sea-gull is a terrible word for a wing-forward because it has connotations which make you seem not quite a forward and it can all relate to a simple decision about whether or not you should go into a ruck.

In New Zealand we operated a system whereby the last man, whether it was a wing-forward or whoever, was detailed to stand out of the ruck on the other side of the scrum-half because we knew that Sid Going liked to break around the base of rucks as well as scrums. We found that this worked very successfully. You can see whether your presence in a ruck is going to help your side win the ball or stop the other side from winning it if you get there after the ruck has formed. And then must come this decision. If they are going to win the ball and I am not going to make any difference then it is my job to make sure that we stop them breaking. On the other hand, if I can help us to win the ball then certainly one has to go in.

There are also these decisions about which way one is going to try to push the opposing fly-half; decisions when and when not to break from a scrum.

What I am saying is that in my opinion the loose forward is more important than a lot of people give him credit for. It might be a conceit but it is a very difficult position to play in and those of us who are in it are totally reliant on the rest of the players in the team to such an extent that their performances can prevent you as a backrow forward from playing well. You can only fulfil half your function if your pack is going backwards.

The other difficulty in this country is, despite what has been said before, that I think our tight forwards are still set-piece orientated. They rarely sprint around the field and they do tend to move from lineout to scrum to lineout to scrum.

I talked about the back row staying on their feet earlier. It is very difficult if you have got to stay on your feet without support from the back for a period of up to five or six seconds. The lapse should never be more than two or three seconds and in that time one can put all one's effort into forming the right base knowing that it is a holding operation until somebody comes.

When you get to the point where you have been holding and waiting and looking round and asking, "Where the hell are they?" eventually there must come a time when you collapse.

As backrow forwards, we obviously feel that we are one of the most important positions on the field, and we feel that we are a little neglected as individuals.

Perhaps I have over-stated our importance, but I don't think that will do any harm. If I can sum up the whole thing with just one phrase, to me a good backrow forward is the one who makes the right decision at the right time. He is not necessarily always the most energetic.

Q. *If you were a coach preparing a side to meet the All Blacks this season, and knowing the sort of dangers a half-back like Sid Going presents, would you choose open and blind side specialists on the flanks? Or would you make them play left and right? And bearing in mind that so much of the All Black lineout compression is done at number six, do you think that your own player in that position should be a hefty fellow?*

A. I think it is very important to play a tall and powerful man at number six who can do this compressing job. It is obviously even more important to do so when playing in New Zealand, where the lineout laws are not adhered to as strictly as they are in these islands. There is no doubt that when Derek Quinnell played for the Lions in the third Test, our lineout return was greater than at any other stage. Derek was the biggest of the selected flank forwards and he did a very good job in this area, compressing at number five or seven, depending on where the ball was thrown.

   I don't think that it is as important in this country, because we adhere to the lineout laws a little more strictly. You have to ask yourself how important is this aspect of play relative to the total involvement. If your ball-winning capacity is not high, you sacrifice something if you have two small flankers. If the front five are good ball-winners, it is not so important to have big flankers.

   If I am absolutely honest, I must say that I think that one of the flankers ought to be a big man but whether he plays blind side is another question. Again it depends on his abilities. Derek Quinnell was somewhat inexperienced at playing in the back row but he did a specialist job very well in that third test.

   It even worked well in defence because the All Blacks like to bang a man down the short side from the rucks, and even though your number six might not be so fast as other flankers, he can get on the blind side and do a good holding job.

Q. *In this lineout compression we have heard about, is there any particular point of pressure that the Lions concentrated on?*

A. The point of the greatest pressure must go in opposite the man who is jumping for the ball on your side. The All Blacks in 1967 and when Wales toured there in 1969 gave the best possible examples of this practice. I can remember Colin Meads just standing there and catching the ball without needing to jump at all because everybody else had been held or cleared out of the way. On occasion, he even caught it two-handed!

PLANNiNG FOR A POWERFUL PACK

By *Ray McLoughlin*
(Blackrock College and Ireland)

You are listening now to donkey number four. This donkey business began, as so many other things began, with the man himself, the "King", Barry John. Towards the end of the tour on one occasion he is reputed to have said that he did not really know what the forwards were doing in there, but whatever it was, the ball came back a hell of a lot and he would like to say, "Thank you."

Barry had very definite reservations about the necessity for forwards in rugby at all. He was particularly hard on me and every second morning at breakfast he was prone to come down, put his hand patronisingly on my shoulder and say, "Tell me again, Ray. Are you a loose-head donkey or a tight-head donkey?"

I see these papers, which are being delivered not as lectures but rather as exercises in which players who have been around for a number of years, in some cases a very long time indeed, give forth the distillation of the experience they have acquired. These views inevitably, therefore, ought to be of some value. If Willie John McBride, for instance, feels after his 55 caps and three Lions tours that it is still a useful thing to give your opponent an elbow in the teeth before you go up for the ball, then that counts for something.

What we say as players, however, is influenced by our own personal assets, opinions and perhaps even prejudices. Ian McLauchlan, for instance, scored a try in some God-forsaken match in the North of Scotland four or five years ago and ever since he thinks that front row forwards should be able to handle the ball as well as backs. I would ask only this. Where do you get the ball for all this handling? Nobody ever gives it to me.

I felt that there might be a case for diagramming on a blackboard the purpose of rugby and deriving from that the importance of forwards. However, I felt that if I did that I would be less than honest because that sort of thing cannot be done on a blackboard. I feel it would be better to set down what I think is important at the moment.

I would like to concentrate mainly on two things. Firstly, on what I believe are the most important factors of forward play. In selecting them, I have done so not because one factor is more important than another but because I feel that some of them just need more emphasis at this time because the return on effort is greater. Then I would like to consider the implications these factors have on training and forwards.

In my view it is essential:

(1) To go forward in the set pieces, particularly the set scrums.

(2) To practise set-piece defence until you are blue in the face.

(3) To continually let all players know what it is hoped to do next.

I have to be loyal to my ilk and say that I think that the most important thing for forwards is the scrum. I would have never gone on any Lions' tours if there wasn't such a thing as a scrum.

Therefore, in the interests of other players who are afflicted, as Ian McLauchlan and myself are, with a particular size and shape and level of skill, I must say that I think that the scrum is the most important thing about forward play.

The scrum is the more organised of the two set-pieces, so most effort at planning attacking moves should be tried here. However, moves will fail 90% of the time if you get the ball going backwards. Therefore, go forward on your own ball and observe the corollary, which is to go forward on the opposition ball so that they are going backwards and therefore find it difficult to launch attacks.

Because going forward is so vital in the set scrum, there is a premium on the type of packing that contributes most to going forward. This means the loose head should get under his man and lift a second or two before the ball comes in, rather than stay up from the beginning, in order to give his hooker a good view. By far the best type of hooker for this type of loose head packing is the right foot hooker because this means he can turn towards his left and get down and up with the loose head. Therefore always pick a right foot hooker. To gear scrummaging to suit the hooker is subjective and not necessarily best.

If I could make a check list for scrummage practice, I would suggest:

(1) The loose head must get under his opposite number.

(2) It should be arranged that scrum-half does not put in the ball until the loose head gives him the signal, because he should wait until the loose head has got the optimum position.

(3) The scrum-half should give some prior signal to the loose head before he gives the signal for putting the ball in, so that the loose head can lift and reveal the ball to his hooker.

(4) Second-rows and back rows must grip the man in front of them really tightly and use their biceps. They must NOT just rest on their feet. Biceps should be completely tensed in every scrum. This helps to mould the scrum into a solid unit instead of a number of parts such as links in a chain. You cannot transmit force by pushing a chain.

(5) There should be a minimum of 30 hard scrums every training night.

(6) Everybody must think of driving the opposition back.

Remember that the line-out is less organised than the scrummage and that most referees know very little about the realities of lineout play. In any case the laws constitute a complicated shambles which bears no relation to realism and commonsense. Therefore if Team A always tries to keep to the law while Team B tries to get away with breaking it, Team B will always win. Consequently, a major objective should be to break the laws where it is suitable to break them while giving the impression that you are not. To this end, players should stand close together so that the referee cannot see so easily what is going on, and the lineout jumper should never bend down to help him jump. The assistance he gets is largely psychological and there is the adverse effect that it reveals the activities of the players on either side of him to the referee. The jumper should never stand outside the lineout to jump in, either, because he loses on two counts: referees tend to penalise him for jumping in, and it makes it easy for an opposition player to slip into the gap so that when the floating jumper connects with the man with feet firmly fixed on the ground, the jumper will lose. He will bounce off and automatically leave a big hole in his lineout.

Blockers should not bend down towards their opponents, because they cannot see the ball coming in and what they do may turn out to be stupid, and they are inviting a punch in the face. What is more, to most referees they appear to be adopting an aggressive pose and referees tend to whistle them automatically. These blockers look as if they are in a powerful position but the man standing up can easily knock them aside using his forearms.

As far as the referee is concerned the centre of the lineout will be halfway between the top of the head of the man bent down and the hip of the man standing up. Thus the near foot of the man standing up will be within inches of the advantage line and the near foot of the man facing forward will be up to two feet away. And remember that the position of the feet is the critical position for the application of power.

I would remind you that it is not the responsibility of the props alone to block a lineout. There is only one correct approach to blocking a lineout. Assuming the last forward stays loose, there are six gaps to be sealed, and if one player jumps, six players are available to seal these gaps. Every player behind the jumper is responsible for the gap in FRONT of him not for the gap behind him. Every player in front of the jumper is responsible for the gap BEHIND him and not in front of him. The traditional text book description of wedging and blocking in lineouts is inappropriate to present day conditions.

It is generally better in lineouts to take the ball down and drive forward thus developing a maul, because the opposition forwards are dragged in and prevented from cluttering the field. Also your backs can close the ten yard gap and therefore render less time available to the opposition forwards for cluttering the field. I must add that the most important part of a winger's play is throwing the ball into the lineout. This should take up to 50% of his time at training. I would also say that too much time is practised on the peel. It is rarely very effective.

If the opposition attempt a peel, the principle must be to nip it in the bud - if possible on the opposition's side of the gain line. If you have decoded the opposition's signals and you know that a peel is about to be attempted, each of your forwards should try to hold his opponent's togs or jersey. If that is not possible, he should follow the ball around. At the same time, your forwards at the back of the lineout should jump and try to mess up the throw, either by knocking the ball straight back up the line or by harassing their jumper. It is also quite useful to "dump" their jumper heavily once or twice, but care should be taken not to do this until after he has delivered the ball because the referee's own list of priorities will have him following the ball and the play, where he will be watching for knock-ons and off-side. Done well, this will dampen the jumper's enthusiasm.

The tackling sequence to be used against a peel is quite simple and it should be decided beforehand. The best way is for the loose forward at the back of the lineout to go hard for the first opponent to receive the ball from the jumper. If he does, he will always get him before he reaches the gain line. The site of this first tackle is the essence of the defence, so any attempt by the opposition to obstruct it should be dealt with decisively.

If you look at the last Lions' tour one of the things I thought that was significant was that the strengths of the Lions were strengths which it was not easy to counter.

(1) Scrummaging ability.

(2) Naturally developed skills that flowed from the team as a whole but particularly from the backs.

It is not easy to counter an effective scrum. If you are coming out second best in a scrum there is not much you can do about it. You can do something, but not much. It is always a plus to the side that has superior scrummaging power.

John Taylor mentioned the second Test against the All Blacks at Christchurch where the back row tended to be sucked in, but that was a temporary error which could be corrected quickly.

The general ability and flow and continuity from the Lions' backs was again something which you can't do that much to counter given that the platform for possession is already there.

The strengths of the All Blacks on the other hand could be countered more effectively because they seemed primarily to be concentrated in the ability of their scrum-half and back row to move from set scrums and in the overall ability of their forwards to drive in the loose.

Good tacklers and well organised back row defence can tie up even the best back rows, and driving play in the loose is something which depends a lot on the success of the point of primary possession. And as I have said, since the Lions were stronger in the scrum, this was something which meant that the opportunities for developing this driving play by the All Blacks' forwards in the loose were limited.

Another point about this is that when you are moving on to the ball as the All Blacks' forwards were, you are prone to make mistakes. You bump into other players for accidental offside, you can have knock-ons, forward passes and so forth and every time you do that you concede a scrum and you are back again to base one and the question of the Lions' primary strength. I mention that to give support to my view that at the end of the day I would rank the question of the scrum as the most important.

There could be a tendency now I feel to think that rugby in these islands is on the crest of a wave and to say that now we have got our scrummaging right and so forth, let's have a bit more running from the forwards and let's have a bit more of Ian McLauchlan's passing. While I agree with that to an extent I would make the point that the All Blacks, as a nation of rugby players, fell into that trap after 1967 of thinking that the whole of rugby was about this 15 man running game and so they had a period of four or five years when everybody was concentrating on this - when you had back row forwards being made into front row forwards with the consequence that scrummaging in New Zealand deteriorated seriously and nobody out there noticed it because it was deteriorating everywhere at the same time and it was left to us to go out and exploit it.

It takes a while to recover from a trend like that. It will be interesting to see how much they have recovered when they come here this season. One of the feelings I had was that they were not quite sure what was wrong with their scrummaging. I watched them at a few training sessions and I got this impression very clearly.

The second thing which I feel is always a top priority is the question of tight defence. Every score the opposition does not make is one which you don't HAVE to make and I think that the view which prevails sometimes that to practise and to be good at set piece defence implies a defensive attitude is really idiotic. When the other team has the ball, there is only one thing to do and that is to defend unless it is to be considered to be attacking rugby to actually let the other side score.

This applies to forwards and backs but it applies particularly to the back row and I think that it is now and always will be a top priority.

The third thing that I feel is now and will continue to be a top priority is that teams should be simply organised. I think that people get hang-ups about this question of organisation. The view abounds that being organised is being constrained. I just don't agree with that. I think that the more options that are available to a captain on the field, the more flexible he can be. The only limitation on the ability of the team is really the captain's ability to call the right moves at the right time. If he wants to call some particular move he cannot do it unless it has been practised and unless it has been given a title so that he can communicate it at the point where he wants it done. It follows that I think there is a priority for organisation in all teams at all levels.

This gives the captain greater flexibility. Remember he can always resort to the supposed blessed freedom of no organisation at all by calling no moves and giving everybody his head. However, the reverse process of going from the state of blessed freedom to the state of organisation is impossible. Thus there is greater inherent flexibility in having pre-practised moves available. The idea that the reverse is true is a common fallacy. Therefore pre-practise and pre-organise. With pre-practised and pre-organised moves the game becomes only as stereotyped and patterned as the captain allows it to be. It is up to him to use his moves effectively and not for the sake of using them. A prime example is the wheeling of the scrum when the opposition is putting in. If the opposition is dominating the scrum it may be the only recourse left. However, it is impossible to wheel an opposition scrum unless there has been considerable practice beforehand.

In the last Lions' tour our forwards did not play well in the first match against Queensland. A major factor was the tiredness that resulted from our long trip but I also felt that Willie John McBride as leader of the pack had an insufficient number of options with which to control or alter the game. We had not practised wheeling for instance which might have been effective at certain times, and after that game Carwyn concentrated for a couple of weeks on this question of increasing the number of options open to the forwards and of organising the play around them and the signals for them.

I remember in 1966 when I was captain of the Irish team, I concentrated a fair bit on this organisation, perhaps too much and people got hung up about the fact that it was too complicated. As so often happens in these situations it became a bit of a joke and Willie John McBride who was one of my best friends, with whom I got my first cap, didn't help by the fact that from time to time he would take the pipe out of his mouth and say, "Lads, will someone tell me what McLoughlin is talking about?"

I consider that a captain can improve his performance enormously by sufficient attention to the following points:

(1) He should imagine the game before he goes on the field.

(2) If he is in charge of a training session, he should plan beforehand what exactly will be done during that session.

(3) He should be objective in his team talks. He should not give team talks just for the sake of giving them. He should not say anything unrealistic or unnecessary.

(4) He should not try to "inspire" the team by shouting and urging if he is no good at it. Rather he should lead by using the controls, reminding players of their immediate tasks and urging only when necessary.

(5) He should be the fittest player on the team. You cannot lead from behind.

The skipper of a well organised team will find it difficult to go on the field with less than 40 or 50 signals, moves and possibilities in mind. However, the player leading a team for the first time will be in trouble if he has to search through forty or fifty items every time the whistle goes for a set-piece. Such a player can simplify this problem considerably by sitting down on the morning of the game and spending an hour or two picturing all distinguishable set-pieces and bringing to mind the pertinent three or four considerations for each one. He can get himself to the point where the relevant considerations only will come to mind and come automatically in all cases.

I think that this idea of developing a "hate" before a game is crazy. Instead, it is important immediately before a game to reiterate plans and signals, because this gets the player's minds on the task ahead and the more the player's thoughts are occupied with the task ahead the more alert he will become, the more quickly he will react to situations in the field and the more efficiently he will contribute to team performance.

I feel that a club captain or a man captaining a representative team which he has led several times before should cut down his team talks to a minimum because players become tired of the same voice saying the same things in the same way.

Some captains and pack-leaders believe in fiery, death-or-glory urging on the field. I personally do not like it partly because I can't do it well but partly because I don't think it is the best way in any event. If it is not done well, it is a futile exercise. Furthermore there are some players who are never receptive to it or who are at best indifferent to it. I believe that if planning and organisation have been sufficient, the best type of leadership is in directing and keeping the players alert by reminding them of what is likely to happen next, for example in scrums and lineouts. The actual realisation of plans is the best motivation of all. If the plans are not being realised the skipper must identify the trouble and possibly change his plans. And finally I feel there is rarely a case for shouting. I think it is always better to talk quietly to players. If you talk nonsense, it will come over as nonsense whether it is loud or quiet.

The captain or coach should establish clearly in his mind what exactly will be done in a training session before that training session starts. He should plan to avoid players hanging around and he should leave set-scrums till last so that the backs do not have to hang around while the set-scrums are being practised. If he manages training efficiently he is seen to manage it efficiently and this is psychologically good for the players. They feel they are taking positive rather than floundering steps towards improvement and they will respond more enthusiastically. This is a motivation in itself.

The job of the coach and the captain is principally to take steps to ensure that for a large proportion of the time, fourteen players on the field know what the fifteenth is going to do and that this knowledge is used to cause all fifteen players to continually apply their energies towards the achievement of the same immediate goal. One of the big differences between the All Blacks and the Lions in 1966 was that the All Blacks knew fairly precisely what was going to happen immediately on the completion of every set-piece, when they had the "put-in". They moved and acted correspondingly and this resulted in efficient utilisation of their resources. The Lions player on the other hand had to make his own individual guess at every scrum and lineout. The great sin was not so much that he often made the wrong decision but that all the players did not make the same decision. Confusion and inefficiency inevitably resulted. If a backrow forward sees his fly-half with the ball and does not know what he is going to do, he just has to guess. He may guess that he will pass along the line to his wing. He would therefore run across the field towards his winger ready for a breakdown or ready to support a break. If having embarked on this journey, the fly-half suddenly kicks deep towards the touchline that the flanker is running from, the flanker looks an idiot. He is wrong-footed and running hell for leather away from the point of play. He is lost to his team for the remainder of that loose play. So are any others who guessed as he guessed. Any opportunity that may have existed is lost.

How much better if everybody knew what the fly-half intended? The flanker would be 20 yards nearer the ball. To say that to arrange that all know what the fly-half intends, is to curb his natural inventiveness, is nonsense. If he sees a wide open opportunity he can change his mind at the last minute but this will be the exception. The game is not designed to have 14 stooges trundling around wondering what some dilettante prima donna in the fly-half position will do next, but rather one where the efforts of all 15 should be combined in the optimum manner to achieve the ultimate objective.

Communication is therefore essential. This involves people and signals. I see the two major factors in this to be first of all knowing what your own players and colleagues are like, what their habits are and the kind of things they are prone to do. I think this is important, very under-rated and something a team can benefit from very much. And the second area is simply knowing what moves are called, whether they are called by the backs, so that as Geoff Evans said when you get out of the scrum you don't have to spend the first ten yards' running time looking around to see where the ball is going. You know the minute you just stumble out of that scrum which direction to stumble towards. One of the strengths of the Irish team in the last two years is the fact that so many of the players have been playing each other for ten or fifteen years and they know each other's play very well. Whenever I get a ball in a loose scrum, Willie John McBride just steps out and waits for the next scrum because he considers it 100 per cent certain that the ball will never come back!

I remember on the last tour again one example of this business of lack of dialogue between forwards and backs was the occasion when Sandy Carmichael got the ball round the front of the lineout and started running across the field. The defence was up particularly fast and they kept pushing him across. He found himself in a position where there was nothing he could do except pass to Barry John. Barry John kept running away from him and didn't want to take the pass and the length of the pass got longer and eventually he got the pass out and Barry deigned to catch it, but that night Barry announced that he was never, ever again going to take a pass from any front row forward like Carmichael or myself. As far as he was concerned he was taking the ball only from Gareth. Gareth's role in life was to give the ball to Barry. He was destined by God to do so.

I feel that the importance of mauls needs emphasising more at the present time than perhaps anything else. I remember Carwyn saying that the ruck is no longer as important as it was some years ago and that this was one of the reasons why the All Blacks have suffered. The change has been brought about by a couple of changes in the law. While I agree with this I think that the maul is becoming more important as the ruck becomes less important, and I feel that whereas a ruck more often than not tends to be a situation which has developed in the open field following a lot of movement and is a thing from which the ball should usually be given to the backs because the opposition is disorganised, many of the mauls are either very static in that they go on for a long time thus giving the opposition backs time to re-organise, or they are the direct consequence of a lineout in which case the opposition backs never got out of position anyway. For mauls of this type the vulnerable point is at the back of that maul because there is no organised defence. Therefore, I feel that there could be more emphasis on developing attacks by moving the ball away from these mauls. I can imagine Mike Gibson thinking to himself that I am trying to generate a reason for my taking a ball from that maul. I can also imagine him thinking - because he has often said it - that when I do take the ball from a maul, he never gets it. But I do think that this is an important area to develop. If there was a weakness in the 1971 Lions' team it was that we were not as good as the All Blacks in taking the ball away from a static maul and creating that initial break.

The opportunity for a forward to create that break stems from the very nature of the way you defend from a maul. You've either got one forward or a scrum-half standing in defence at the side of it and I think it is very feasible for a large percentage of the time for one forward to move up with the ball, hold the first man off and slip the ball to his scrum-half who is then through. Once he is through, he has outflanked the cover. There is no cover coming from the forwards. He has penetrated behind the backs straight away and I think that backs have more freedom of movement from this initial break by a forward than they would have otherwise.

I will qualify the remark I made about this possible weakness in the 1971 Lions by saying that when you have backs of the quality that the Lions had on the last tour, you obviously should move the ball from mauls even though there may be mauls where you would do it much less than you would if you had backs of the type the New Zealanders had.

Because teams in Britain have had better backs over a period than New Zealand, it is only natural that New Zealand forwards generally should be good at this phase of play. More has been required of them in this matter than has been required of forwards in Britain and therefore the All Blacks should be better at it, but I do think that this is something that we should develop.

This implicates not just the attitude towards it but it also requires us to develop the ability of forwards to run and take men out of the game in the way that the All Blacks do.

The second point which arises from this is the matter of how you get the ball out of a maul. Too often, at all levels, players go into mauls and they all start mulliking for the ball. If one player was to just catch the hand of the opponent with the ball and just pull it back the ball could be taken very easily. The Welsh forwards about five years ago had a particularly neat habit of giving you a dig in the ribs or catching you in the mouth or a few other niceties like that which were really very effective at getting the ball away from you. I would not advocate that but I would advocate a consciousness of thinking about what you can do to get the ball from that one opponent. After all, eight players should be able to do it if they surround him properly and all of them should be thinking of the best way to just take the ball off one player as they are running into the maul. It is a matter of consciousness and I think we do not have it sufficiently.

The next thing which I think is very important for forwards is this question of not following up attacking moves. I agree with Ian that it is important for forwards to take and give a pass, not because I think that they should be used necessarily as attacking players, rather than forwards, but because they are going to get in the way of moves very often. If they are going to drop a pass or make a mess of giving a pass then the fitness which got them there in the first place is a liability rather than an asset. For this reason, if no other, I think it is important that every forward who is likely to be able to get in the way of attacking moves should be able to take the ball and pass it as well as anybody else.

This came to me on the Lions' tour more than it had done before. Carwyn got the forwards to warm up for half an hour using the ball all the time, and I think that the improvement in the handling ability of the forwards was remarkable as a result. It didn't have much effect on me because I had certain physical short-comings like not being able to bend or twist or run, but in general it was of enormous benefit!

This is of tremendous importance. It is hard enough to generate moves from which scores can come, and so often you see a forward getting in the way, and he just stumbles along and drops the balls or he gives a wild overhead pass and the whole thing breaks down. It is necessary sometimes to be there as a link, but the forwards should be able to link better rather than worse.

The next point which I feel is very much under-rated is the matter of not giving away penalty kicks. I am supposed to be a complicated guy so I thought I had better try to live up to that, and I have worked out a few sums based upon the assumption that you have two teams equal in ability and that when they play each other, neither team will score a try. Then make the further assumption that they are equally prone to give away penalty kicks and that in the course of the match the referee will give six penalty kicks that are very kickable. Say you have Barry John on one side and Bob Hiller on the other and so you know that they are nearly certain to kick those six penalties.

Well, after all that, it may surprise you to know that the odds are only 31 per cent that the match will be a draw at three penalty goals each. The probability is 69 per cent that the penalty goals will be split 4-2, 5-1 or 6-0 and the probability is that one team will score six points more than the other through penalty goals.

Now, if you go further and assume that one team is better than the other by one try and you have the other conditions still applying, then the scoring of that try will make no difference to the winning of the match. The team that has the six points from the penalty goals does not need the try and the other side still won't win.

Therefore if you have teams that are fairly closely matched, it is realistic to say that you are working towards a one try advantage in ability more often than not, and if what I say is true it follows that in that situation - which at top level is fairly frequent - you are wasting your time with all the effort to be a better team for 69 per cent of the occasions.

Now I think these figures are meaningful. I also think they are real and they state that if your coaches and teams apply priorities in the right way the first priority should be absolutely and totally to prevent the players from giving away penalty kicks. Secondly, the priority should be to concentrate on how you trap the other side into giving away penalty kicks, and thirdly the priority should be to develop a goalkicker like Barry John and Bob Hiller to take advantage of those opportunities. All this business about scrums, organisation and forwards and backs is less important by far.

Now what do you conclude from this?

As I have said, the first thing you conclude is that the lineout laws are a disaster, and as long as they are, the second conclusion you draw is that it is utterly important that you put a lot of effort and a lot of thought into not giving away penalties and trying to get the other side to give them away. I feel that this business of giving away penalties is something that is very hard to get right. You can go out on the field and say we are not going to give away penalties but you give them away and it is the same the next game. The business of trying to develop a consciousness about not giving them away is very hard, but it is very, very important if you want to win matches.

The last point I would like to make concerns detail in the lineout. Now I always found this business of standing on the jumper's toe a very useful little trick. If you stand on his toe just before he goes up, it is not only not so easy to go up, but he looks down to see what is happening and the ball hops on his head and he certainly doesn't get it. I remember in the Welsh-Irish game in Cardiff last year, I was trying to stand on Delme Thomas's toe and

Delme started shouting at me, and he kept moving back further and I kept moving back with him and he kept trying to jump like this and it was a quite ridiculous situation. Willie John McBride burst out laughing in the middle of the match. When you think of it, with Barry John and Gareth Edwards out there with all their skill and their ability to plant the ball on a sixpence and score tries, that you have two apes like us mucking around like this in the lineout, it is ridiculous. But what do you do about it? As a realist you have got to accept the fact that you are an ape relative to Gareth Edwards, Barry John and Gerald Davies. However they need the ball from the ape who can ape better than the other guy and therefore you SHOULD step on the other guy's toe and pull his hand down and so on.

I have gone through eight points which I think warrant emphasis about forwards; scrum, lineout, tight defence organisation, knowing what will happen next, use of mauls, don't foul up attacking moves and don't give away penalties, at least not in lineouts. The three things which I feel tend to get less emphasis perhaps than they ought to get are the use of mauls, don't foul up the attacking moves and don't give away penalties. Every attacking move you foul up is a try thrown away. Every penalty can be extremely significant.

I have jotted down what I consider to be the priorities for forwards resulting from the consideration of these eight points.

First the matter of the scrum and tight defence and organisation generally is essentially a coaching responsibility. There is not much the player as an individual can do about it except contribute where he can to the overall coaching exercise.

The main things for the forward himself to do:

(1) Observe his fellow players.

Players' habits are very important whether it be the way they go into rucks, the way they turn, the way they give the ball back, whether they give it to the first man in support or whether they prefer to wait for the scrum-half. If you come up to a player whose natural tendency is to wait for the scrum-half you will only muck the thing up if you fight him to try to get the ball off him. If, on the other hand, he is a player who wants to give the ball to the first man coming in support and you assume that he is going to give it to the scrum-half you stand there like a Charlie when he gives you the ball. You also waste valuable seconds while you cotton on to it. So study your fellow players. It is something that you can spend years being vaguely aware of and yet not really absorb that much in the way of detail. Only so much will automatically sink in.

(2) Be fully briefed about organisation, signals and moves. At club level, this is often not done.

(3) Think as you go into mauls.
You can talk about doing this but when you get into a match, you just forget about it. The trick here is to try over a period, to develop a consciousness and that is a hard thing to do. One of the most difficult things in coaching is to try to develop this consciousness in players, but if a coach has to try to do it for the player, a certain amount has been lost. A bloke can think about it and work at it and kick himself in the pants when he realises that at a given maul he did not think as he should have done. The more he kicks himself in the pants the more he will create the habit of thinking as he comes up. The player also has to decide what choice of play he should make from the maul. You have to decide whether it is the kind of maul from which you switch the ball out to the backs or whether it is the kind of maul you drive on from.

(4) Developing a consciousness about penalties.
This is very important. Attention to lineout detail can help a lot here. It is important to avoid giving the impression of doing the sort of thing that can be penalised. As I have said, it is crazy to lean forward and lower your head when you are blocking. It is crazy because it gives the impression of aggression and the referee tends to watch you more. It is a pity that this should be so because you gain nothing for it. This is an

instance of grimy, uninteresting detail that Barry John
would never want to know about.

(5) Handling.
I think the ideal way for a forward to improve his
handling is the sort of warm-up sessions with the ball
that Carwyn had. I think that everybody should do it.
I am sure that not enough is done about this, certainly
at club level.

Now having considered that check list, I want to discuss its
implications for training.

What is it that determines the total training programme over
a period of time? The importance of the various factors I have
mentioned is one, but it is not the only one. Return on effort is
important. The fact that it is probably more important to
practise scrums than rucks does not change the fact that beyond
a certain point, the increase in benefit that you get from this
does not warrant the time spent. There is a point when you
should change from the top priority things to the lesser priority
things. There is a need for variety, obviously. There is a need
for aggression, too. Not enough attention is given to this in forward
practice. There is a need for the kind of training that will develop
aggression like, say, Rugby League practice, in which forwards
take on opponents and try to knock them aside. We in Britain
are bad at shrugging off tacklers and retaining the ball. Our
body position is bad, and so is the use of our arms. Our timing
is wrong. New Zealand forwards are much better than we are,
and a spell of practising with the Rugby League three tackle rule
would help us.

Finally, something which again I consider is understated is the
need for strength training in forwards. Forwards are usually
strong people. Even little fellows like John Taylor are strong, and
given that you can get so much from an efficient scrum, it
is important that you spend a bit of time on weight training;
push-ups, with men on your back, which can exploit the basic
strength that you've got. Anybody who has done weight training
knows that in six weeks he can improve his capacity enormously.
I am no expert, but I know that all you have to do is to exploit the

basic potential which is there in a strong man by getting the co-ordination of the muscles right. Some time should be set aside in one training session a week for a fairly heavy workout; squatting with two guys on your back, maybe; sets of fifty push-ups, and so forth.

Now much of what I have been talking about can be assessed on the basis of what return you get from the effort you make. If you take a club side which has not been together for long, the return on effort in trying to get the initial organisation right can be very high and very marked in the first few weeks.

You are still a long way from realising the potential in the team, but you can get the level up quite a lot in a short time, therefore team organisation is something you should always get right first. If effort is concentrated on getting moves, signals, co-ordination and organisation right, you can improve the initial level of performance in defence. You can improve it quite dramatically, although organisation does not have nearly as much effect at improving the attacking potential of the team.

Once the organisation has been put right, there is a fair amount of opportunity to actually practise and execute basic moves. Having the signals to do scissors moves and bring in the extra man and so on is one thing. Their success depends on the basic ability. Given that you have a certain stock of skills initially, one can improve the utilisation of these skills by a period of practising on them and you can get a good return on effort on it by concentrating on that for a period of something like four weeks.

The toughest area of coaching as I see it is the area beyond that. At that point you have got the organisation right, you have had a fair amount of practice at your various moves but you have to guard against all this organisation being a bit of a constraint.

Therefore, the next job is to try to get players to break free from these restraints. This is a very delicate thing. There is a lot of art in it. You can be banging away at it for some while without much success and then suddenly the fruits begin to come. I see it as a business of trying to develop naturalness and spontaneity, of releasing skills and of confidence. I don't think that there is a set way of doing this. It is an imperceptible thing, but it comes eventually.

On the tour, Carwyn used to talk about coaching at the conscious and the unconscious levels. He used to say that the Lions had a particular ability to play at the unconscious level; at least he talked about that up to the Canterbury match when it took on a new meaning! He dropped it from then on.

He used to talk too, about operating in second gear. I remember in the earlier games in New Zealand, he said that we were operating in second or third gear and one of these days everything would come right and we would click and explode and be in top gear and I think that Carwyn himself holds the view that the day this happened was against Wellington. I think it is a characteristic pattern when you take a team from scratch you spend a while when the fruits of the various things you are doing to get this spontaneity thing right just don't come, and then suddenly they do come and you reach a new plateau.

I think this might be a basis for debate and it is also the reason why I think that no matter what skills you have in your team there is a case for spending a fair amount of time initially on organisation and on getting the basic moves right. The four week period for practising moves is perhaps too long because there is an inter-relation between the periods involved.

I have a great respect for Carwyn as indeed everyone has and I felt that on the Lions' tour he was good at all these facets of coaching. Lots of coaches can do the early parts but the subtle business of releasing the naturalness and the spontaneity which is an artistic thing is much more difficult and I think that that was the thing which he did particularly well.

I would now like to put before you some rules of thumb that I think apply in forward training consistent with the points of emphasis that I have already made.

(1) Organisation and set-piece defence. Get it sorted out early and quickly.

(2) Early emphasis on the practice of drills.

(3) Gradual change to the development of continuity and flow.

Other features that I feel should be built into a training schedule are a half-hour warm up with the ball, an average of 70 scrums a week, regular weight-training of one night a week, occasional practice at mauls like in Rugby League but not too much because this business of practising pulling players' fingers in mauls can get boring.

Finally, I would like to discuss this question of unopposed team training. I have always felt that unopposed practice is basically wrong, particularly for the forwards, because to suddenly stop in the middle of the field when somebody calls "ruck", then turn around and get the ball back, is such an unnatural thing to do.

I remember that in Australia in 1966 we practised this religiously for a while. Against New South Wales, one of our forwards suddenly got a ball when he was facing his own line and he started to run backwards. Now he didn't see that there was nobody behind him but we did and running backwards seemed a most ridiculous thing to be doing. One of the opposition thought so too and came up and hit him a dig in the kidneys and he was out for two minutes. I thought that this was a consequence of the training we had done when there was a tremendous emphasis on stopping and trying to generate a ruck artificially. I feel that the emphasis should be on going forward and letting the scrum or ruck or maul develop naturally. Too much unopposed, if it has this element in it, creates bad habits.

On the last tour we did not really have any unopposed. Carwyn always managed to drag out some sort of opposition even if they were only invalids, amongst which I usually was. This provided an opposition so that rucks developed naturally and it was not necessary to call them artificially.

However, you cannot always have that situation. There are other reasons why you should have unopposed practice and where you have to accept the habits that can result. You must have periods of practice when forwards work with the backs and practice that communication between them which I see essentially as the backs letting the forwards know what they intend to do when they do have an intention. Whenever this is raised, the backs usually say, "But I don't want to be bound to do this or that." You are not binding them to do anything. All you are asking to know is if the captain or the leader of the backs has stated an intention because this does mean that there is a higher probability that the intention will be tried.

The other justification for unopposed practice, of course, is that backs need to simulate match situations and this is one way to provide it for them.

I consider that rucking is over-emphasised in coaching sessions. You may have 60 lineouts and 30 to 40 scrums in a match and often not more than 13 or 14 loose rucks. Clearly the game is dominated by set-pieces. Besides, all things being equal, a loose ruck will be won nine times out of 10 by the team that created it. You cannot create loose rucks until you are effective in the set-pieces. It is a truism but nevertheless bears statement that nearly all loose-play follows a set-piece. It is not surprising therefore that the extent to which you can exploit loose play and breakdown situations is largely governed by the degree to which you can influence set-pieces. When they are working well the team develops confidence and the remainder of the game slips into place far more easily. If you spent all your time practising basics and practising scrums, you would finish up doing better in the rucks than you would if you spent all your time practising rucks and no time practising basics and scrums and lineouts. Therefore practice of set-pieces is of considerably more importance than practice of loose rucks, until the set-pieces are operating efficiently.

If in doubt a player can never go far wrong by putting his head down and going as hard as he can at the opposition. Players too often are criticised for this. This is because the philosophy of hanging around for a pass is too prevalent. If there is sufficient close support, and if the player going forward is taken down, the supporters are in a position to get in and ensure the ball comes back on the correct side. If a player puts his head down and is tackled and grounds the ball and if an opposing player picks it up, the tackled player looks a fool. It is not his fault but rather the fault of the lack of support. The bloke who shouts "Thick forward" is very likely one who doesn't know what he is talking about.

As I have said, once a player's habits have become established, particularly at a higher level, the best thing to do is to observe them so that you can fit in with them, but if the players involved are younger and more easily moulded, then the important thing about rucking is to know which technique is going to be used, so that the supporting players know what is happening in front of them. Let me enumerate five possibilities.

(1) The player with the ball goes down on the ground so that his body is between the opposition and the ball. The supporting players then drive over him.

(2) The player with the ball turns his back on the opposition and holds it until the other forwards are wedged around him. He then feeds the scrum-half.

(3) The player with the ball turns his back on the opposition and slips a pass to a supporter, who drives on. The process is repeated until the movement is stopped and then the ball is fed back.

(4) The player with the ball turns his back on the opposition and waits for a supporter to take the ball off him. The process is repeated until the movement is stopped and then the ball is fed back.

(5) The player with the ball drives forward with his head down and leaves the ball either on the ground or on his trailing hip for his support players to carry on the drive. When the movement is stopped the ball is fed back.

Now if the support player thinks that he is going to be given the ball, as in example (3), and the ball carrier thinks that the ball is going to be taken off him, as in example (4), then the support player will never get the ball and will over-run.

Therefore, there must be prior agreement about technique.

Which is the best technique to use? Definitely number 5. Much could be said about the shortcomings of the first four alternatives. I would say just this. The idea of stepping over the ball as in the first method just does not make sense to me. There is no power in this situation and the player on the ground will get hurt.

Turning the back on the opposition is also unsound. As I have indicated with the example from 1966, if the ball carrier has not connected with the opposition, he is a sitting duck. He can also be turned round, and because he cannot see what is coming, he is powerless to prevent this. An opposition player can slip round to his front and hang on to the ball and refuse to let it go and because he is jammed there by the arriving forwards, he cannot be penalised. In addition to all this, the man turning with the ball can be hit in the kidneys, he can be tripped or scragged backwards so that the ball can go anywhere, and he can also be thumped and possibly hurt by his own players.

Using technique number 5, the man with the ball should go like a ding-bat and as he runs into the opposition he should put his head down and his shoulder forward. The ball is not held to his stomach but at his side or hip. He keeps it away from the opposition. When he finds himself finally stopped, he hits the opponent as hard as possible and down low and leaves the ball on the ground or on his trailing hip. His momentum will carry himself and all he has connected with a few feet forward. His job is now done. The support follows 4 to 5 yards behind the man with the ball, not any closer. When the support finally sees the carrier checked, they accelerate, pick up the ball or take it and smash forward.

This process is repeated until either the defence is breached and play has opened up OR it has slowed down.

There will be a moment when the support sense that the opposition are tied in and on this occasion they should drive past the ball and into the pile of opposition that has gathered. When that moment comes, the forwards should not collapse. They should DRIVE into the ruck and stay on their feet.

Ideally the carrier tries to hit the opposition and create a vacuum for the ball. The good player will sense when he cannot do this and will flick the ball back a yard or two to ensure that his support can. The support will also sense the danger and move a bit closer. The ability to sense such a situation on the part of both carrier and supporter is developed only by practice.

In the typical contact situation, the carrier drives into opponents with his shoulders down around their midriffs. He is in the powerful position, but obviously, if he suddenly finds that it is sticking out a mile that he should pass to a supporter, he should do so.

In training, scrums should always be done after running. If you expect forwards to contribute in some kind of training which demands running you cannot expect them to do it after 70 scrums. Their sharpness will have degenerated somewhat!

I think that you should also cut down the amount of lineout practice once the organisation is right because they are fierce boring things to be practising all the time. As Geoff said the number of moves you can make from a lineout is really very limited as the laws now stand. As I say, more often than not, peels don't work and so I think there can be too much emphasis on them. I would add this about the lineout though. One of the most important things about not giving away penalties is knowing just where the referee is so that whenever you are going near the line you don't do it if he is looking at you.

Developing a consciousness about not giving away penalties is hard to do but it is well worth working at.

The final point I would make about training sessions for a coach is that he should not fly in the face of what the players believe in.

I have put down a few points that I think are worth making about handling forwards throughout the season. It seems to me to be fruitless to pick out something that a forward has done wrong in a match. I am all for a coach in a training session pulling up a forward if he does something stupid, but it is questionable to start pulling him up about something specific he did in a match. If a player has faults you should talk about them, but it is dangerous to pull him up on a specific incident in a match because it might not be just the right one and there may be factors about it which you cannot see from the sideline.

Another point which is damaging is this "thick forward" implication which comes from much of the comment from the backs. A certain antagonism is built in all the time. The forwards think of the backs as being dilettantes and airy-fairy and backs think of the forwards as being great big thick dummies. A much more effective way of getting the message across to forwards is to demonstrate that the backs only got the ball three times in a match.

I believe there is a case during the season in club rugby to change the pack leader from time to time. If you have a pack leader who is better than the others then keep him for the peak periods. If you have others who can do the job reasonably effectively, then change.

This has a number of advantages. Players get bored listening to the same voice and providing you have built the basic structure of signals there is always room for a change in personal emphasis. This change makes players think about the different nuances and it keeps them on their toes.

I would also like to reiterate that I think it is possible to have too many team talks of the sort where emphasis is placed on hating your opponent and so forth. These just don't work. The need for team talks of the blood and thunder type is becoming less and less as the attitude of players generally becomes more and more professional.

I don't propose to go into the unit practices of scrums and lineouts. I have tried to cover the general role of forwards and the implications of these factors on the programme and schedules of training.

Finally, I would like simply to consider the All Blacks' tour which is coming up. First, I would say that the All Blacks are not dummies. They will have given a lot of thought to the exercise of last summer when the Lions beat them, and I think they will come here as a much better team and may well surprise us.

The one area where I feel they might not have recovered sufficiently is in the matter of scrummaging, because as I said earlier I got the impression that they did not quite know what was wrong. Because their scrummaging had degenerated over a period they were not quite sure what it was that caused the difference between their scrum and ours.

The second point I would like to make is that I don't think that the All Blacks' forwards will be bigger than ours despite the various mentions to that effect which have been made. Agreed Muller was much bigger than Ian McLauchlan, but if you put down the weights of the packs it just does not work out. People think of the giant Colin Meads. Well, Colin Meads is only 15st. 12 lbs. At one stage of the Lions' tour, all four of our lock forwards weighed between 16st. 4 lbs. and 16st. 12 lbs. stripped. They were all bigger than Colin Meads. So to think of them as "the big All

Blacks" is a bit of an illusion. They are unlikely to be heavier than international packs here. However, I do think that they will be a lot better and we should be aware.

We may criticise the All Blacks for being slow to react to the way that the Lions played in New Zealand, but remember it was only over a period of one New Zealand winter and rugby in these islands has taken an awful lot longer than that to react to the facts of life which have been presented to us over the many years when New Zealand and South Africa teams were always putting it over on the Lions and other teams from these countries.

One might say of the All Blacks that they have never changed their pattern over the years. Well, it has never been necessary for them to do so because they have been able to stuff everybody over the years. It was the right pattern for the most part for them in the light of the laws as they existed until recently.

We should be slow to jump to the conclusion that they will be slow to learn. I think that they will learn a lot quicker than it is generally thought.

Q. Do you think there is any value in wheeling the scrum?
A. I have never been too enamoured of the merits of the wheel in attack, the traditional Scottish type of wheel where you turn the scrum and have the lock forwards moving away. I don't think that it is significant, but what I do think is significant is the wheel of the scrum in defence.

If you are not able to push the other pack off the ball very quickly, or if the opposition has a particularly effective back row, it can be very effective to exercise a violent wheel just as the ball comes into their scrum. You have your own scrum-half picking the very earliest moment when the opposition are putting the ball in. He shouts some monosyllabic word at the top of his voice and everybody then violently tried to wheel, with the left side going forward the right side coming back. By doing this, you can completely wreck the opposing scrum. Apart from the fact that it puts all the tight forwards on their backside, it has the advantage of destroying the co-ordination of a team that is geared to back row attack, because they are uncertain about offside and when they should break. The two wing forwards in the pack doing the wheeling should step out and kick the hell out of the ball as it comes out of the other scrum. It is a destructive thing, but it can be effective. It does need a lot of practice to get it violent enough. If it is not violent, it can be a liability.

The attacking position for the loose head on the opposing side's put-in. The loose head has got underneath the tight head's rib cage and has taken him down to an uncomfortable position in which he can exercise no control with his shoulder. The loose head is then ready to thrust upwards by straightening his back and driving with his legs.

Tight-head scrummaging on his own side's put-in. The tight-head (right) keeps the opposing loose head outside him and drives to the left with his left hip to push his hooker as far to the left and therefore as close to the ball as possible.

This position represents disaster for the loose head. The tight head has wrapped the loose head underneath his shoulder and bent him inwards.

This position also represents disaster for the loose head. His feet are too far forward and he is bent almost double so that it is impossible for him to transmit the shove coming from behind him.

Q. *Ian McLauchlan talked about packing straight. Ray McLoughlin used to be a destructive tight-head prop. Now that he is a loose-head does he think that the tight-head should prop straight or be destructive by boring and lowering? Was it not the result of Sandy Carmichael's boring in the Canterbury game that the trouble started off with Hopkinson?*

A. Dealing with the last question first, I do not think that the problems in the Canterbury game resulted from Sandy Carmichael boring. Sandy Carmichael in my experience, does not bore in. He scrummages straight and hard and brings the scrum down to the level his hooker wants but he does not bore. The punch-up against Canterbury had to do with other factors altogether.

On the question of whether the tight-head should bore or lower, I have never agreed with this business of boring in on the hooker. I never did it myself when I was playing tight-head because a good loose-head can get in under you at an angle and lift you up and render you powerless. This is what Geoff Evans was talking about when he said that if you have tight-head who is boring in he starts off at an angle and the more the lock pushes, the more he forces him out.

Against a good loose-head the tight-head could be in dire trouble. He can be switched around at right angles to the tunnel of the scrum.

I do think, however, that just as a loose-head can create immense damage as our loose-heads did in New Zealand by getting under their opponents and lifting them, so it follows by definition that it is extremely important for a tight-head to counter that. The way to counter it is to go down fairly low. I am not saying that the tight-head should put his opponent on the ground, but he wants to try to keep him under his shoulder and under control. The secret of this is very simple. If a hooker demands, as most hookers do, that they must wrap themselves around you to get a feeling of tightness and comfort I think you have to consider that tightness and comfort for their own sake are not necessarily right. What you want to achieve is a certain end result.

Your best chance of doing that as a tight head prop is to bind in the manner which is probably loose enough to break the law, but in such a way that your left shoulder is loose and so that you can increase the gap if you want to. You start off by being in with your hooker, but you are not held by him and then you just go out at the last minute so that you bring your loose-head in under you and when you've got him where you want him, you can move back into your hooker and tighten up again. You wrap the head of the loose-head under your shoulder and stop him from getting in so far that he can lift you up. So that I agree with that kind of destructive play but I do not agree with taking the scrum low enough to collapse it. You want to keep it high enough to push forward and to make the loose-head helpless.

Now, on the loose-head side I agree with Ian that your back should be straight but it does not have to be parallel to the ground. I was watching Muller before the first Test practising scrummaging against Colin Meads and Colin Meads was pushing him. The reason he was pushing him was this. Meads had his legs back and his back was a bit bent and Muller had his feet dead straight and he was packing dead straight. Now ANYBODY could have pushed Muller in that position because there was no flex in his body with which to apply push. The position he was in is thought of as being a good pushing position, but that is an illusion because it is good only to transmit push from your second and back row. That's not enough nowadays. You've got to have the prop pushing as well.

A prop, a loose-head particularly, needs to get an initial lift so he should start off with his legs a bit bent and with his back perhaps angled down a bit, not too much, but just a bit so that at the right time he can lift and get a certain amount of flexion whereas if he starts off in what should be his finishing position after his thrust, he has nothing left to give, so while I agree with Ian that a prop's back should not be curved, I don't think that it should be quite parallel to the ground. Ian himself does exactly that. His back is straight, but slightly angled, and at the right moment he brings it up level and then on a slight upward incline.

Carwyn James. This story broke some days after the first test. I believe it emanated from the All Blacks' hooker. I did not accept the premise then and I still don't. If a prop is boring in consistently, the scrum becomes very loose because he is being pushed out by his lock. Our scrum was never loose. Indeed, this was the very thing we were most concerned to avoid. In every training session, whether we did 40 or 50 or 70 scrums, we made sure that every scrum had to be really tight.

Q. *Is there any advantage in packing 3-2-3 rather than 3-4-1 when using an eight man shove?*

A. I don't think so. A 3-2-3 formation is useful for setting up a back row move, but I hold the view very strongly that the 3-4-1 formation gives the most push, because the flankers can contribute so much more and they are so important in getting this push right. The difference between a good wing-forward scrummager and otherwise is very marked. On the Lions' tour, we had tremendous wing-forward pushers; every one of them was good. If props do not have good wing-forward pushers behind them they cannot direct their own efforts at all. Their whole effort has to be concentrated on trying to remain in position and not to be split away. Loose-heads particularly need to be kept in a fair bit. We can apply ourselves a lot more if we are kept in by the flankers.

Binding is also very important. I think that the biggest difference between the All Blacks' scrum and the Lions' scrum was in the binding. Binding on the inside leg is very important.

This came home especially to me in watching the All Blacks' practice in the first test. Their locks bind round the outside leg of their props and it is a most unnatural position, because you have to cock your wrist to keep your elbow up. As Geoff Evans says, the arm in front of the chest is a much more powerful position. It is much more effective at keeping the prop in and it has the added advantage of enabling the lock to maintain contact between the backsides of the front row and his shoulders. The importance of this is not really appreciated. You can only hold weight and transmit through a really solid contact. If there is any looseness, you get a chain link effect where you have a lot of loose pieces and you cannot transmit power through a chain. And above all that, I don't see how a second row can get any sort of push if he is going to keep his arm far enough round the outside leg of the prop to let the flanker in to a pushing position. The lock slips over the prop more often than not, particularly if the front row is packing low. If the lock's arm binding is low enough to be effective, he forces the flanker to push in the back of the prop's knees, which does not help at all.

Carwyn James. The New Zealand scrum bound round the outside legs, and this stopped them making the best use of the shove of their very powerful flankers.

Q. *Did you have any signals for co-ordinating the shove?*
A. Nothing special. On an eight man shove on the opposition ball, the pack leader called a signal. In our case it was the name of a back-row forward. The scrum-half then shouted to us at the earliest moment, and we all worked to that. Practice is essential to pull it all together as a really explosive thing.

Q. *How did you channel the ball through the scrum, and did you try to bring it across to the far side away from the opposition scrum-half?*
A. A conscious effort at channelling never seems to work. The return on effort is not that high. The key to it is the way the ball is put into the scrum and how the hooker hits it. Other things are more important. The first essential is to get the ball and the second essential is to go forward. You should not sacrifice foot positions too much in order to get a certain channel. If the ball has been struck incorrectly in the first place, it is not easy to get a channel. It depends on the co-ordination between the scrum-half and hooker as to how far the ball comes into the scrum before it is hit. If the hooker hits it early rather than drag it back, he is going to tend to knock it out of the side of the scrum. Then you depend on the prop

and the flanker to fish it back. On the other hand, if the ball goes into the tunnel further, which it tends to do with a right foot hooker, there is a better chance of getting it back at the right angle and along the right channel.

THE FLY-HALF AND THE CENTRES

By **Mike Gibson**

(N.I.F.C and Ireland)

Let me say at the outset that all of us backs have been very impressed with what the previous speakers have brayed! While the forwards were talking, I had a chat with John Dawes and we reckoned it was a good job that William Webb Ellis first ran with the ball and that 15 players eventually became involved in the playing of the game, otherwise the backs would have had a good chance of some form of redundancy payment and the forwards would have had to be reported to a Monopolies Commission!

When I was listening to the forwards talking about compression and standing on each other's toes and retaliation, it seemed to me that there was not much room for skill!

Therefore, I am glad of the opportunity to talk about fly-half and centre-three-quarter play, because I can move at once to a person whom I consider to be one of the most skilful players in the game, and for that reason, I am glad that Barry John is not in attendance, otherwise it might inflate his opinion of himself!

I am sure that the fly-half is the person who reflects the attitude and the potential of any team of which he is a member, and no one did that with more individuality and with a greater sense of character than Barry John. His ambitions had very few limitations and the challenge and the stimulus this provided for his fellow Lions went hand in hand with a psychologically crushing effect on the opposition. Very few fly-halves can have daunted so many opponents as completely as Barry John.

It goes without saying that possession is vital and that nothing can be achieved without it, but it is essential that you have a player at fly-half who is a player of quality. The higher his quality, the richer are the prospects of the team as a whole.

I have listed the qualities which I think are essential in a fly-half.

(1) Handling ability. His hands must be sure because he must have the confidence of his forwards. Nothing infuriates the forwards more than the fly-half dropping the first pass, so the pack must be quite content that the fly-half's hands will not waste any possession, and that he will be able to pass the ball effectively.

(2) Kicking ability. Too often, a fly-half is limited if he is not sufficiently well equipped both to kick and to pass. He must have a full range of kicks. He must be balanced in everything he does, balanced both physically and mentally.

Now handling, kicking and passing are mere words, but if you have any ambition to play rugby football to any level, you must be prepared to practise until these simple skills become second nature to you. They should not even enter your mind consciously at all. That then leaves your mind completely free to evaluate each situation and to express itself by translating the options which are open to you.

From the time the 1971 Lions were in Eastbourne, there were distinct signs that there was immense potential in the backs. It was just a question of whether we could express that potential.

Carwyn believed that a ball was the inevitable requisite for acquiring facility with a ball. He was not a dictator, he was an artful persuader. He made us work hard and he made us train hard but he always gave us a ball to play with and the more we played with the ball the more it became an extension of our arms.

This meant that when we went out to play in a match, we were sufficiently practised in handling to keep mistakes to a minimum. With that confidence, we were free to express our ability, free to handle the ball from our own line, free to attack from any situation on the field that offered us the possibility of doing so. The success we achieved was due purely to our constant practice and to our constant use of the ball in training. Possibly the greatest weakness in training sessions from schools to first-class club level is that there are rarely enough footballs on the field.

In considering the handling of the Lions, I was very disappointed to read that Terry McLean, in his book on the tour, said that Barry John was the worst passer he had ever seen at international level. Now having played outside the man, I would argue about that to the end of my days. I think that the style of passing is shifting nowadays, and Barry's style is in the modern concept which is simply to get it there; it doesn't matter what you do as long as you deliver the ball in a catchable position in front of the receiver. I will vouch for the fact that he did this very effectively.

In former days - when John Dawes was starting his career! - we had the old notion of the English public school hip-swing pass, the true delivery, with the body swaying one way as the ball goes the other so that the opposition is committed by the swing of the hips. Now there are still times when this is the right thing to do, particularly when you have developed a situation where you have a 3-2 overlap and you really want to take somebody out. I would point out that if you study enough photographs of Barry John passing the ball, you will find instances of him doing just this.

The true delivery, with the body swaying one way as the ball goes the other... If you study enough photographs of Barry John passing the ball, you will find instances of him doing just this.

His other method, though, was to give a top and bottom hand roll pass, like the French. If he took the ball up on his shoulder, he just flicked it on with his hands. If he took it low, again he sometimes just flicked it on. It was more of a wrist pass.

The only thing Carwyn insisted on was that every time we passed the ball down the line in practice, we had to keep uppermost in our minds the need to put the ball in a catchable position IN FRONT OF THE RECEIVER. He would follow behind us, harassing us, shouting, "Think! Think! Think!"

Now once the back-line had acquired the ability to do that three times, say when Barry John put the ball in front of me, and I put it in front of John Dawes and John Dawes put it in front of the wing, with each pass delivered to the right place, then anything was possible. It may sound simple and obvious, but it is true.

I can assure you that if one pass went behind the shoulder of the next man, the feeling of failure among the Lions' backs was such that Carwyn didn't even have to say anything. So when a fly-half makes a pass, he must make sure of putting the ball in front of the next man, because if he puts it behind his hip or up behind his shoulder it just reduces the possibility of what can be achieved. And rest assured that fellows like John Taylor can come past you in a match and give you a fearful rollicking for an avoidable error, an error which can be avoided by practice and concentration.

The more we played with the ball, the more it became an extension of our arms...

Have a good look at some matches next season and see how many passes are bad, how many passes are high, how many passes in fact rule out the possibility of an attack developing. You will be surprised.

The other point about a fly-half's play is his defects. As I said at the start, his character really reflects that of the team, and consequently, his defects are mirrored in the performance of the team.

As soon as some fly-halves come under a certain degree of pressure, they slide in behind the scrum or behind the lineout. Again, look for this in the matches you watch. You will see a fly-half move in behind the set-piece instead of holding his position. HE will be all right. HE will be protected, but his very position requires him to run across the field. That is the only way he can avoid the flankers, and the more the fly-half runs across the field, the more the rest of his backs have no option but to do the same. This is one of the worst features of fly-half play, and it is one of the most prevalent.

The fly-half's job is as a link. He takes the scrum-half's pass and coordinates the team. He is the player who gets the first bite at most of the possession and it is vitally important that he makes the best use of that ball.

When I am playing fly-half, I find that there are certain points that I try to be aware of during a match.

CONCENTRATION

I think that lack of concentration is a defect at all levels of the game. Lack of ability to devote yourself entirely to the game for 80 minutes. Too often, in club matches, you will find fly-halves having a look at something in a miniskirt and white boots.

At international level, I only feel satisfied if I come off the field feeling mentally tired. I must feel mentally shattered because you must be able to direct all your thoughts to one object and that is: What is going to be the best use for this particular ball?

Now when we talk about concentration, that in turn leads on to other things like alertness. The effective player is the one who looks alert, who looks the part, whose mind is active, who is considering the possibilities, who is considering the strengths and the weaknesses of the opposition. Only by total concentration can you acquire the speed of thought which is so necessary, particularly at international level.

If you get hold of a ball and go on the field and think, "What did John Dawes say?" "What did Mike Gibson say?" then you will be lost. You will be trampled on. You might even come within the range of fellows like Ian McLauchlan and Ray McLoughlin, who, believe me, are fellows we backs should avoid! So speed of thought and speed of reaction are essential to a fly-half. Your decisions in that position must be precise, and they must be accurate because you are not going to get too many bites at that ball and therefore the more you misuse possession, the more inflated an ego the opposition loose forwards will get. They will see what is happening and say, "Right. They've made the mistakes. Now it is our turn to try some attacking moves."

So if you want to guarantee a continuous supply of possession and to encourage the forwards to provide it, then make good use of the ball. Otherwise the boys up front will either lose their enthusiasm or they will deny you the ball.

APPRECIATION

This is tactical awareness. Standing there and appreciating what are the strengths in your own team and what are the strengths and the weaknesses in the opposition. This awareness extends to your surroundings, to being aware of your position on the field and the possibilities it offers and also to being aware of the state of the match.

PATIENCE

If you concentrate enough, you will develop a form of patience, like a cat waiting for a mouse. Particularly as a fly-half, the player who can lull the opposition into thinking he is either predictable or a fool often earns a big reward.

In Ireland, so many people talk about Jack Kyle, but they don't talk about him only in Ireland. They talk about him in Wales too. Cliff Morgan illustrates his own career very well with a story about Jack Kyle.

Cliff's first international for Wales was against Ireland and he had heard about the great Jack Kyle and was all ready for him. However, during the match, nothing much happened and Cliff began to think, "Who is this fellow? He's not doing anything. He's just taking the ball and putting in the odd kick; passing the ball along. A well equipped player, a good footballer, but nothing like as good as his reputation."

Cliff confesses that he became a bit confident and he relaxed and suddenly, Jack Kyle was away and he scored. It was one of the great tries of the game and it was scored by Jack Kyle in Cliff Morgan's first international.

So develop a patience as a fly-half and you will find that wing-forwards will relax slightly. Then if you are alert, if you are aware and if you are practised, you can make them pay for that moment of relaxation.

Attitude

This point was best illustrated for me in New Zealand by Barry John. It was fascinating to meet someone like the King because his attitude when he went out of the field was not to worry about what the opposition were going to do. He was only concerned with what HE was going to do and he believed that anything was possible. He had this composure about him. He had concentration to a standard where in fact he was relaxed, or gave the impression of being relaxed. I remember Bob Hiller saying that when he captained the side once, he was quite sure that Barry did not listen to a word of what he was saying in his team talk. He was just building up his concentration in his own way. Yet Barry's mind was extremely active and if there was any defect in the opposition, or any opportunity, it was never a case of opportunity looking bigger in retrospect. Barry was a player who saw opportunities coming. I certainly found that by playing alongside him, my vision became broader. Above all, he was the player who personified the attitude of the 1971 Lions.

A fly-half needs that positive attitude. He needs to be confident. He even needs a touch of brashness. When I was at Cambridge, I remember Dr Windsor-Lewis saying to me that when he went out on to a field to play, he would look around and see the wing-forward in the opposing side and think, "Poor bastard. He has to mark me today."

This is the attitude a fly-half must develop, but he can only develop it if he is supremely confident in the simple things of catching and passing and kicking.

Don't get the impression that rugby football is a vastly complicated game. I would say that the one thing at international level which shows up repeatedly is the fact that there is a lot of pressure on players, and a lot of pressure on the back line and if you get a ball and see an opening and cannot take a pass and give another in one or two strides then you won't live, because the pressure and the speed of the game will be too great for you.

Therefore, it is worth while for a player to concentrate on doing the simple things well, and I will preach this until the cows come home. Once you develop the ability to do these simple things, then you can step up in level from club to county to international to British Lions, and because you have mastered the basics, you will have equipped yourself to tune in gradually to the speed of your new surroundings.

So the fly-half must be a player of immense vision. He must be a player who is wise before the event. If you watch a really good player operating at fly-half, you can sometimes marvel at his vision.

DEFENCE

In defence, I see the fly-half as an organiser. He has two different tasks to perform, one from the scrum and the other from the lineout.

From both scrum and lineout, however, the fly-half's first job is to bring his line up; to give his own defenders a line in defence. This line in defence is essential. More teams give away tries through bad defensive alignment than you would believe possible, even at international level. We have had some notable examples recently.

The fly-half must also give assistance to his flankers, but this depends on what plan of defence the loose forwards are adopting.

Imagine how I felt as a mid-field player, knowing that I had only to create an extra foot of space for Gerald and he would capitalise on it!

If they have decided on a pincer form of defence from the scrum to attack the opposing scrum-half and to put him under pressure then a much greater burden of defence falls on the fly-half.

The fly-half's first priority is to make sure that his opposite number, or the player who takes the scrum-half's pass, does not make an outside break. For my own part, this is the one point of defence I really concentrate on because if my opponent does make an outside break, it puts too much strain on the cover. It is not so bad to be beaten on the inside. If I come up on the outside and I am beaten on the inside then my opponent is isolating himself from his own supporter and he ought to be cut out by my loose forwards.

There are different types of fly-half in defence. Reference has already been made to the King. At times, he came up in defence and at times, he did not. He read each situation to decide whether to make his presence felt. In the tests against the All Blacks, he would usually go up a couple of times early on to get close to Bob Burgess and make him aware that he was there. Then he would hang off him for three or four times. This made things a bit awkward for the centres but at least we knew what was likely to happen so we could accommodate him.

When I am playing fly-half, I like to attack my opposite number in defence, I have already made reference to the importance of the basic skills and in a way, I am sorry that fly-halves nowadays have that little bit more room in which to move because of the changes in the laws. Players who are quite ordinary have now been given more time in which to operate.

In my days (!) back in the middle 'sixties the defence lay flat and this put a player's basic skills to a more severe test. I find it frustrating sometimes now to see ordinary players being given the time to stand back and kick for gaps or kick down the line. You know quite well that they are not good players, but you can't get any pressure on them. So as a fly-half, I am very keen on pressurising my opponent.

The other aspect of a fly-half's defence is as a coverer. Once you have attended to your opposite number, then you must come across as a form of sweeper to give support to your full-back. If your full-back is a John Williams it is surprising how often that support can provide the opportunity for counter-attack. Barry John had an unfailing nose for that sort of opportunity, either in a supporting role or in picking up a loose ball.

The subject of counter-attack will be discussed more fully later, but I would like to talk about attack in general.

Attack is the translation of possession and pressure into points, and I must stress that possession means attack. I must also stress that attack is possible from any position on the field.

Too often, players try to excuse their lack of ambition by saying, "But I was inside my 25. I know there was a chance of an overlap, but because of my position on the field, I put the ball away into touch."

Again, I have to hand it to Carwyn as far as this was concerned. His theory was that if you had the ball, then you are attacking and providing you had a mastery of the simple things in the game, then you could attack from anywhere. So let me say it again: Possession means Attack.

This point was well illustrated in the Lions' game against Hawke's Bay. Hawke's Bay were leading 3-0 and a chap dropped at goal. (I must just say that Barry John missed touch!) The drop was a marvellous kick from out by the touch-line but it struck the outside of the far post and John Williams caught it on his own line.

Had that been a New Zealander, I have no doubt whatsoever that he would have thanked his lucky stars that they were not 6-0 down and the ball would have been carted away to touch amid great sighs of relief from all the players.

Not so with John Williams. In practice, we had concentrated on getting back in support in depth so that John Williams had an option. He could kick, or he could pass. On this occasion, the player nearest to him was John Bevan but a lot of other players were back and the movement quickly developed. It ended up with Gerald Davies running through between the posts to score a try which we converted to give us a 5-3 lead. So 3-0, possibly 6-0, became 3-5.

That all stemmed simply from the attitude that, "We have the ball, therefore we are on the attack and it doesn't matter a damn where we are on the field of play."

As I have said before, so much of a team's attitude to attack depends on the fly-half. If he is not attack-minded, then the side as a whole will cease to function as an attacking unit, for one depends on the other to a very large extent.

Sometimes, you say to people, "We will play attacking rugby." They say, "Grand" and proceed to run everything from everywhere and imagine that they are playing attacking rugby. The whole game then collapses into a rather frayed game of basketball. I for one just do not like the idea of irresponsible running, even in exhibition games. I favour speculation, but it must be responsible speculation.

A fly-half has three options. He can either pass, kick or have a run himself. If the fly-half is kicking, he must have a wide range of kicks. The chip over the top, the grubber, the high kick, the kick to the wing, the kick back to the box.

The important thing is always to be aware of the options, and then to know which of them to choose. Your head may be full of ambitious schemes but they must be used at the right time. A coach can outline the options in various situations but it is still up to the player to make the correct choice.

As Ray McLoughlin has said, it is much easier, and the return on effort is much greater, to be destructive and to set out your patterns of defence than it is to attack.

Carwyn always referred to this conscious level. He could coach people up to a conscious level but beyond that it was up to the individual, and this takes us back to concentration and alertness and to having a feeling for the game.

In attack, some players are good at set-piece ploys, because they do not have to think and to improvise. Everything is laid out for them.

The Lions' backs had many set moves, most of them fairly familiar in first-class football, but in the end, all of them depended for their success on the players involved reading each situation. The moves were never mechanical. Even with an overlap play, the outside man each time had to read what was on. Once a move had been called, the Lions did not go through with it come hell or high water, whatever the quality of the possession, as so many teams do.

There was a process of evaluation each time and we did not hesitate to cancel a move if we thought it wasn't on.

I remember once in the game against the Maoris, the "King" called a miss move but when it came to it, the ball was so slow that it was not good enough for us to do the move. Barry saw this and did not go through with it. Instead he sparred for a moment, and I supported him close in and was eventually able to cut back out and link with John Spencer. The point was that the "King" had seen that the move was not on and so had I, and without saying a word to each other, we had both taken the correct alternative course of action. It is moments like this that give you your supreme satisfaction on a football field.

Of course, with a player like "Syd" Dawes in the centre, the Lions had a great advantage because his presence meant that the right thing almost invariably was done. His choice of play was as immaculate as his use of the ball.

John Williams' appreciation of each situation was also nearly infallible. He was criticised in his early days for indiscriminate entry into the line from full-back but I can think of scarcely an instance in New Zealand when he did the wrong thing. In addition, his confidence was supreme, like that of the "King". There was no thought of the possibility of an error. And even if there was an error, so what? His attitude was a total contrast to the attitude of so many full-backs of earlier generations who had been brought up on the principle that no one must make a mistake. John Williams' attitude was: Of course it is possible. He only came into the line when the possession was of good quality, but given that essential condition, he was prepared to come into the line from any position on the field. And of course he was right. The cleaner the possession, the more the situation in the backs is four against four and ultimately, one against one. Then there is massive scope to bring in the extra man. Rugby breaks down into an appreciation of what is possible and I think it was here that the Lions' backs held their greatest advantage.

Backs are individuals and the game which is chosen for them should be aimed at releasing their capabilities. I thought that the New Zealand backs were too constrained and because of this they

Every fly-half must have a wide range of kicks…

had not developed their capacity for reading the game and making the best appreciation of what was possible. They allowed themselves to depend too much on Sid Going. He was their inspiration, whether kicking or running.

The player most affected by this was Bryan Williams. As Tony Richards of Lancashire showed in the Rugby Union's Centenary games, when he caught him three times from behind, Bryan Williams may not have had the sharpest edge of speed but he was a most capable runner with great strength of leg and he had a devastating side-step off his left foot. Had he toured with the Lions and worn a red shirt, I have no doubt that the 1971 tour would have established him as a super-star. Yet he was criticised in his own country. It was said that he was out of form. Personally, I doubt that.

When Bryan Williams played such marvellous football in those Centenary games in England, he had Jo Maso and Pierre Villepreux and Joggie Jansen to set him up. In New Zealand, he did not have those players around him, and so he was not set up in the same way. That was the difference. Bryan Williams was a much better player than he was made to appear. A wing may be a greater player in isolation but his ability counts for nothing if he is not given the ball properly, and this is bound to affect his confidence.

Williams played in the centre in the first Test, which seemed rather a waste. He kept stretching across but he was not quite fast enough to beat us on the outside and "Syd" and I picked up some good defensive lines on him so that if he side-stepped he came straight into our bodies instead of into an outstretched arm.

Wayne Cottrell seemed to be too aware of the fact that it was his job to provide the stability and the experience in the New Zealand back line. He became over-conscientious. He was either not willing or not allowed to speculate. He was too conservative. He was much better when he went to fly-half.

Phil Gard did not produce any frills but he was strong enough to stampede at an opposing defence. I had the impression, too, that Ken Carrington had been told to do this against Gerald Davies; to commit him as hard as he could. Carrington tried to do this, but because he had not been set up properly, Gerald tackled him each time. In defence, Carrington looked very nervous against Gerald, but then, so would anyone. Imagine how I felt as a midfield player, knowing that I had only to create an extra foot of space for Gerald and he would capitalise on it!

Mick Duncan also fitted in with the New Zealand pattern at that time. He was a challenging runner. He had power. I thought that all those New Zealand backs would have benefited from the experience they got against us and I thought that they would all have benefited from more liberal thinking, particularly with a player like Bob Burgess at fly-half. The All Black pattern was too predictable, and therefore it could be contained. I am not suggesting that New Zealand could have changed this pattern overnight, but the players they used against us ought to have gained confidence from that experience. Their passing down the line was inferior to ours at that time but they ought to have learned the art of correct distribution and I see no reason why they should not now be free to release their skills. Certainly, Sid Going is a great enough player to change his game to vary the point of attack. If he was required to change, he could change.

With new players, though, the All Blacks might find it more difficult to change because experience and confidence count for so much in back play, and if they find it hard to change their approach to set play, nothing is surer than that the New Zealand backs will find it even harder to change their approach to play from the loose.

Play from the loose is much more demanding, because you don't know how the ball is going to come, you don't know how your attacking forces are going to be deployed and you don't know how the defence is going to be organised. The play then breaks down to spontaneity, to the reaction to situations. You cannot categorise attack from the loose. It is an attitude of mind.

If you are willing to be positive, you can achieve anything. If you are too conservative, you cannot really enjoy the game.

For me the Lions' tour of New Zealand was a wonderful experience because a pattern of play was set up which suited our players. We were given the opportunity to express ourselves within that pattern. Any attacking ploy tends to set up a pattern of play and from experience I find that the variations on that pattern are the ones which bring the scores.

This is where the achievements of the Lions' forwards was so vital. I have played in so many teams where possession was so limited that the backs were trying to play the variations before they had established a pattern.

So attack is first of all confidence in your ability to perform the basic skills, then it is an attitude of mind and finally it is a question of support. When I watch a game, I always like to see how much running is done off the ball.

One of the features of the Lions' attacking play in New Zealand was the creation of the overlap and we found that John Williams opened new horizons for full-back play by his introduction into the line. We found that the best place for him to come in was between the centre and the wing when his line of run was good. I should mention that one of J.P.R.'s own criteria was that the ball should be good in the first place. He was not so concerned about the position on the field. If the ball was good and everything was set up he would come in.

He found that he could achieve a better line of run between the centre and the wing than he could closer in because he could run straighter. This is the difficulty of bringing in the blind side wing. Inevitably, he tends to run across and inevitably, he pushes everyone else across. In addition, if a line is moving at speed it is difficult for the wing to come across field and make up enough ground to get in at the correct angle.

Introducing an extra man is the obvious way of creating an overlap, but it can also be done by good use of the ball. You use a longer pass and drift a bit on the pass and get slightly outside your man. The first man manoeuvres slightly outside, and if the next man and the next work to achieve the same object, the whole thing becomes exaggerated all the way down the line until you have created an overlap. Your opponents may adopt a defensive formation to counter the extra man, but it is much more difficult for them to contain a back line which is capable of using the ball well enough to put a man away.

The same sort of running can also be used with great profit in defence. We often did it in the tests against the All Blacks. John Dawes and I would talk to each other as we came up because I always felt that our back line had the edge over the All Blacks as far as speed was concerned.

I would like to sum up by saying that rugby is like love. It is a game of touch and feel and instinct. It is a personal experience. rugby is also a simple game and you will enjoy it if you master the basic skills and give freedom to your instincts and freedom to the naturalness of the game.

Q. *Was it not Gareth Edwards' long pass which gave Barry John the time and the space to play so well?*

A. It certainly contributed to the success, but Barry was still his supremely arrogant self in the first test in Dunedin and Ray Hopkins played with him then. Now "Chico" hasn't got anything like the same length of pass and to be perfectly honest, Barry is the sort of player who could play well with Harry Secombe at scrum-half!

COUNTER-ATTACK AND THE BACKS

By **John Dawes**

(London Welsh and Wales)

Before I start my talk about threequarter play in general and about counter-attack in particular, I should like to make a couple of points about what has gone before. First of all, my Welsh colleagues would like to assure Mike Gibson that Harry Secombe is a jolly good scrum-half! Secondly, I would like to confess that I have been one of those guilty of calling the forwards "donkeys". After hearing them talk, I feel I ought to apologise. "Apes" would be a better word!

As far as threequarter play is concerned, I believe that given the ability to perform the basics of catching and passing, it is the approach you have in going on the field which determines whether you are a good threequarter line or a bad threequarter line.

Let me read a quotation for you. "The best way to enjoy any sport is to set yourself that nearly unattainable target. There is no greater enemy of efficiency than the attitude which says: 'This is good enough. We have done it enough and we have gone far enough. We have always done it this way. Why change?'

"Perfection in technical accomplishments should come from the belief that you can only begin to think about Rugby when you have mastered the basic skills and mechanical details to such a degree that you don't have to think about them any more and you don't have to be hesitant about them. If in passing and repassing, you go through a trained and purposeful pattern of swift movements then it can become splendidly effective. It can be as exhilarating to the participants as it is entertaining to the onlookers and bewildering to opponents. Understanding and perfection of the skills of running, passing, handling and positional support leads to spontaneity and instinctiveness within the framework of a team."

That is a quotation from a book published in 1967 by Izaak van Heerden, a South African. I think that if we have that sort of approach, that sort of attitude towards our game, we will do well.

I have another quote here which I think is important as far as attitude is concerned: "Pre-match and after match discussions and coaching would centre on the principles of basic rugby, passing at the right time, correct backing-up and team support."

That is a quote from Jack Finlay, who was vice-captain of the Kiwis here in 1945/46. It seems rather surprising in view of the impression we have of dedication to coaching in New Zealand, to find someone from Australasia simply coming and saying that all they ever do is concentrate on the basics. As Mike Gibson said: This is all we ever do. This is all we ever did on tour - to catch and pass, and to devise games whereby we would catch and pass, you could do it without thinking about it.

These attitudes, of course, are essential. What I expect of every player, any member of the three-quarter line and the forwards, is that they should explore the complexities of the game. It is not only the fact that the harder you train brings joy, the harder you think about it brings just as much satisfaction.

What do you go on the field for? Do you go on the field for a game? For enjoyment? Do you go on the field to win? Do you go on to the field to win or to enjoy it? You've got to make up your mind beforehand, long beforehand, why you are playing this game, and I suggest to you that while some of us may have been fortunate enough to play for the British Lions and our respective countries, our attitude is no different from yours. We play because we want to play, we give it a lot of time because we want to, and we do it because out of it we get enjoyment.

The true test of any occupation or profession is that the more you put into it, the more you get out of it. As far as I am concerned, this attitude and approach we had going to New Zealand was belief in ourselves. At no stage did Doug and Carwyn and myself believe that we could not win. We were convinced we could win. We had a belief in ourselves.

As Mike has said, Barry John never thought about what the opposition were going to do. It was what he was going to do. We all felt, "What are we going to do?" Positive thinking. We knew the ability was within ourselves. We knew what we could do, we knew what players we had if we could put them in a position to exploit their ability, and this is what we worked on.

I am a great believer in the rhyme which says, "If you think you are beaten, you are, if you think you dare not, you don't, if you try to win and think you can't, it is almost a certainty you won't." That sums up my approach.

Another thing I believe is this: the fundamental characteristic of all sport is competition, the biological basis of all sport is that people are different. You've heard Ray McLoughlin say how important it is to know the chap packing down next to you. I would say it is also important to know how the chap next to you likes to receive a pass, or how he likes to give a pass. I believe that approach determines what you do on the field. Coaching determines how well you do it.

Barry John's goalkicking was an example of this positive thinking. We did not set out on the tour with any idea that he would break every scoring record in sight with his goalkicking. Indeed, I often wonder what would have happened if it had not been for an incident in the second match of the tour, against New South Wales in Sydney.

We were in a fair bit of difficulty in this match when we were given a penalty kick in the middle of the field. It was pouring with rain and that Sydney cricket ground was so muddy it was like glue. I called Barry up and told him to put it into touch as near as he could to their line. But he put it down and kicked a goal! Cheeky monkey! I never thought he had the power to kick a goal from there. It was out of the worst of the mud on the cricket table in the middle. That was positive thinking! It told us something that we did not know about Barry John, and it probably told him something he was not quite sure of himself.

Over the ages we have proved that we can produce the best three-quarters in the world. We do not always use them as well as we ought to but we do produce them. If one looks at history, you will see outstanding players coming out time and time again. In the '60s we tended to slump a little bit because of the attitude towards life perhaps, as far as the people concerned who were playing rugby. I remember that when I left school (one or two years ago!) and branched into first-class football, there was no 10 yard gap between threequarters at the lineout. You could stand as near as you possibly could to the gain line, which dates me somewhat, and I realised very quickly that from a set piece it was virtually impossible to score, unless someone made a mistake and let either you or them through. You relied on mistakes - such were the laws of the game. The introduction of the ten yard law has created more space but nevertheless I still maintain that it is still impossible to make a break against a good, organised defence unless they make a mistake. Therefore other ways had to be found, and for a long time we did nothing about it.

We reduced our type of three-quarter play to ten man rugby because we were afraid of making a mistake behind the fly-half and let's make no mistake, forwards are the first to condemn you if you do make a mistake behind the fly-half, and quite rightly. There is nothing more depressing in rugby as going backwards. So instead of trying to think of a way around it we resorted to ten man rugby.

There are other ways, there were other ways but we were not prepared to explore these complexities of the game - certainly not in the back division so we became rather stereotyped.

New Zealand, with their Ian MacRaes, thought of one way of breaking it. The big type of centre taking the tackle to create a ruck, etcetera, and then we all tried to copy that, instead of thinking of something of our own, thinking for ourselves and using the ability we had.

It was just before the touch kicking dispensation law came in that we started to see the way ahead. Attacking full-backs and over-lap play came in. One or two clubs in the country - Bristol if I may mention one, started using this overlap and movement of the ball, but there were clubs still reluctant because of the attitude of "You must not lose" rather than "You must win", to let the ball move beyond the fly-half unless he was kicking to the wings, in case a mistake was made which cost you a try or something would happen which would cost you the game. Then, the dispensation law came in for an experimental period and it has made people think about the possibilities. The law itself has not, I think, made such a significant difference, but it has made people think: If you cannot kick, what can you do? We should have done that before the dispensation law came in. Anyway, it has brought the role of the attacking full-back to the front. Fortunately we (that is my club, London Welsh, and Wales) happened to have almost the ideal attacking full-back, so we exploited it. Several clubs have since tried to play an attacking full-back. You can get away with it for a while but, against a really good side, a full-back has to be a full-back. He will be exposed if he is nothing but a runner.

I feel a full-back should have three qualities in addition to those qualities we all know a full-back must have. He must have courage, concentration and anticipation. I am sure you will agree that John Williams certainly has those three, anticipation being the key factor. Lots of full-backs come into the line not half as effectively.

Anticipation! When to do it! Is that something we can coach? I am not sure - I believe it is innate. This, undoubtedly, was one of the major factors why the Lions succeeded in New Zealand. Since we came back people have been talking about the overlap game. All I will say about the overlap is that it is an effective move and, as I am sure Ray McLoughlin would agree, it is an option. It is not something you go out and do every time you get the ball back from the forwards - it is an option.

In New Zealand we had twenty-five options behind the scrum. We had the overlap and 24 other options provided by Barry John, none of which they could really solve! I must be honest, we seldom tried anything except the overlap in the backs because most New Zealand teams were so preoccupied first with Barry John and then with Gareth Edwards, that when the ball did come out and we did try the overlap, it was almost always effective.

We found that the best place to bring John Williams into the line was outside the centre, because there, he could run the straightest line at the greatest pace. The full-back's angle of run and his momentum are crucial to the success of the move.

John Williams did not come into the line unless it was a good ball, but given that first essential, he was prepared to come in from almost any situation on the field. As far as the move itself was concerned, J.P.R. would not start his run until the ball was in the fly-half's hands. Then he would go as hard as he could so that he was overtaking the line and going through on the burst when the ball reached him. He had to be going flat out at the moment he received the ball, and this meant that the first three passes from the scrum-half to the inside centre and on again, had to be swift and accurate.

So

(1) We had to have a good ball.

(2) J.P.R. delayed his run until the fly-half had the ball.

(3) The scrum-half, fly-half and the inside-centre each had to make a quick and accurate pass.

(4) J.P.R. had to time his run so that he was accelerating to achieve maximum momentum when he received the ball.

Once he had done this, J.P.R. had to set up the man outside him; to make sure that he timed his pass properly. This is the sort of judgement which only comes from practice.

Then, having made the pass, J.P.R. would go on backing up, and supporting his winger, right to the end. Sometimes he would get a pass back inside. Sometimes he simply had the best view of all of the winger running in to score. He says himself, somewhat ruefully, that he got passes back far more often from the right wing than the left!

In all the set moves which involved John Williams, he tried to achieve these two objectives, to run the straightest line at the greatest pace.

Of course, we had many other set moves. The various "miss" moves, in which one or other of the midfield runners was missed out by a long pass. We called those by the name of the man being missed out. "Miss Syd", that was me; "Miss Mike"; "Miss J.P.R." and so on. We also used the "miss" move which was first evolved in South Africa, with the wing coming inside his centre. Again, this move had the great merit of straightening the line, and "Ally" Biggar pulled it off several times really well.

We also had the various "Rangi" moves, which have now covered the world. These are the scissors moves named after the

New Zealand player Ron Rangi who first produced them against the Lions in 1966.

The idea originally was for the outside centre - or centre, as they call the player in New Zealand - to take a scissors ball from the fly-half, or first five-eighth, with the man in between missed out. We used that move, and also the same move produced closer in and initiated by the scrum-half. We called that move the "Arthur".

We called it that because Arthur Lewis did it very well. Gareth Edwards would run away flat to the open side of a scrum and instead of passing to Barry John, he would give a scissors ball to Arthur Lewis running inside him from the centre. We brought off this move as clean as a whistle after half-time against Canterbury. Arthur went in and touched the ball down without a hand laid on him and it sewed up the game. We also used a dummy version of the move. We used a variety of split moves, too, in which the backs are split 3-2 from a scrum, with the added alternative of bringing in the full-back on either side. The dummy drop at goal and then move to the short side and give the ball to John Williams. This set up a try for David Duckham in the second Test at Christchurch, but the referee said a pass was forward. It was also the move which enabled John Bevan to equal Tony O'Reilly's record number of tried scored in New Zealand, because it produced that elusive 17th try for Bev in the match against North Auckland.

Incidentally, the North Auckland scissors combination was easily the best move used against us in New Zealand. That scissors sequence which involved Sid Going and his brothers Brian and Ken from full-back and fly-half was so good that I am sure it will be adopted and evolved all over the world.

Canterbury produced a couple of interesting variations of the Brian Lochore No. 8 move from an attacking scrum, but instead of taking the ball out to the backs, these moves kept it among the forwards. The move in which the number 8 did not give the ball at all, but in the end turned and went for the line himself, almost produced a try. Fortunately, Mike Gibson's defence was equal to the occasion, even though he did have a very large lump on his head as a memento!

We did not use the loop, or the double, very often in New Zealand, although Mike Gibson did bring off a beauty against

Wellington. We did make a fair amount of use of the crash ball, though; the short pass given to a man running on a straighter line than the general diagonal drift across the field.

Several alternatives are possible with a crash ball. The fly-half can give the ball to the outside-centre coming inside, or the inside-centre can give the ball to the wing doing the same thing. If you introduce the full-back to these moves, the extent of the variations increases.

Basically, though, we found that the overlap worked more consistently than anything, and we found that it was not so much the length of Gareth Edwards' passes as the speed with which we moved the ball that created the overlaps. As Mike Gibson has said, the essential was to place the pass in front of the catcher.

It is also essential to have a full-back who is a REAL full-back. It is not enough to convert a runner from another position. You might get away with this for a match or two, but eventually, he will be exposed.

Mike Gibson has given an instance from the Hawkes' Bay game as an example of counter-attack, but again, how do you make a chap counter-attack? Can you put him into a position where you drill him, for want of a better word, into a counter-attack? I think the answer, in most cases is, "No", because how would he react under pressure? He will react under pressure in a way that is natural, and it is your natural counter-attackers who do the unexpected.

The secret of counter-attack is not only having someone like that, who has this innate ability, but in having five or six people around him who are able to read what he is going to do, and react to it. You can coach running back, support play, all this is essential. The fitness to do it is essential, but I do not believe you can coach how you do it.

As Mike has dealt with attacking play, I should like to talk about the role of three-quarters as far as defence is concerned. I am a great believer in having someone in your side who has the ability to crash-tackle, who can catch a man in possession and really knock him over, but the way the game is going at the moment, players like this are very, very few and far between. If you have one you are extremely fortunate. Use him. But if you haven't a crash-tackler and it is not a fault of the people concerned - then you must think more seriously about your defence.

How are you going to defend from set play? As I have said already, I don't think the game has changed that much in the last ten years. We have learned how to combat the Ian MacRae type of play. But how do you combat the overlap, which is an option?

I quite honestly believe that there is no answer to the overlap. There are some answers which will work for a short period during the game, but there is no ideal answer.

There are three schools of thought on defence to the overlap.

The first is to bring the full-back into the line to take the opposing full-back.

The second is to let the attacking full-back come through to be tackled by one of your midfield players while your wing stays out to cover his man.

The third is for the winger to come in and for the full-back to cover across. This method, incidentally, does not have a lot to commend it, because it has conceded some fairly spectacular tries!

We tried to combat the overlap when it was used against us in New Zealand by simply talking to each other as we came up in defence and by having complete reliance on our back row and half-backs to stop an attempted break or break inside us. We then adopted a line of defence in such a way that we could cover one or two men simply by talking to each other and shuffling across, so that we were overlapping ourselves. Then if someone came through on the overlap, one of our mid-field players could get him.

We also concentrated on the role of the wing. What does the open-side wing do? Does he come in, or does he stay out? We asked our open-side wing to stay out with his wing, to block off that route, to stop that pass, so that when the full-back came through, he came through on his own. It was then a question of getting to him quickly, and the nearest men to him are the mid-field players.

I've seen other people try other things, like bringing a forward out for example, and parking him outside the outside centre of anywhere he thinks the full-back is coming in. If that happens, then you are one short in front, and that can be exploited by the other team so that I don't see that is an ideal answer.

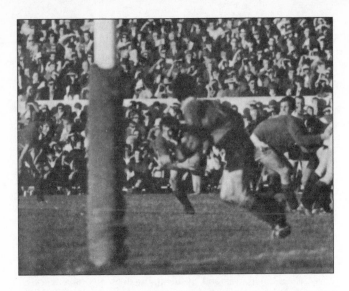

Gareth Edwards runs to the right of a scrum against Canterbury to begin the Lions' move called the "Arthur". John Bevan's disinterest on the left betrays his own lack of participation!

The move ends with Arthur Lewis appropriately putting the ball down for a try without a hand laid on him.

The other possibility, of course, is to use the blind side wing. What should be his role? If you bring the full-back up and use the blind side wing, it leaves an awful lot of ground which can be exploited with a kick. As I said, I see no answer, no ideal answer to it.

At the moment I think it is something that British rugby has contributed to the modern game, and it is for us to exploit it and next season it is for the All Blacks to try to stop it. They might well succeed - such is their dedication, such is their knowledge. They might well find an answer, but I don't think they had one while we were there.

Youngsters want to go on the field and they want to play like Barry John and Mike Gibson and they go out there and try to do the things they see Barry and Mike doing, but they should realise that Barry and Mike practise catching and passing so that they can do both naturally without thinking.

Mentioning Barry and Mike and saying that they practise their catching is rather a misleading statement. Barry achieved tremendous success with his boot out in New Zealand, as we all know, probably because he seldom would come with us to practice catching and passing. He always used to take a soccer ball and practise in some goal-mouth, somewhere or other! But great, he could catch and pass and that was all we asked him to do.

I would also like to say one or two words about captaincy. Captaincy these days is difficult. I am not going to say what you should expect of a captain or look for in a captain. Let's take all that for granted. It is an opinion anyway. Can I simply deal with the captain in relation to the coach and the pack leader, assuming that the captain is in the backs. And despite what John Taylor said about captains in the backs only calling back row moves once every other season, I still think that the backs are the best positions from which to captain a side.

Coaching is now fully established in this country, but it is essential for both the coach and the captain to work in harmony and that their fields should overlap. The captain helps, when required to, with training; the coach helps the captain with the tactics of the game. After all, we must remember that it is the captain on the field who has to make the decision at the time.

I am very much aware, as you all are, that we must not think that if you appoint a coach to your club he can provide all the answers. You must not expect him to be able to give you five or six priorities to achieve to win a specific match. As Carwyn showed in New Zealand, if you are going to be successful it will be because of the contributions of the individuals, what they think about and how they react. What Carwyn did was to select the best material available and put them into practice. I think this is the role coaches ought to adopt. They should make sure that every player in a side is used. All players should feel that they are needed both to play the game and to think about it.

And finally, if the captain is in the backs, then do not interfere with forwards. Let them get on with it. We are very selfish people in the backs. All we ask of our forwards is to give us the ball. We don't even ask them to run and pass, because we know that is beyond them! We simply ask them to give us the ball. We are gradually getting to the stage where forwards CAN run and pass but, as Ray McLoughlin rightly emphasised, "Let's have our priorities right." Forwards are forwards, whose job it is to be ball winners. We as backs primarily are ball users, and if you are going to have harmony within the framework of the team, and if you have a pack of eight forwards fighting like hell to make sure you are in possession, then you must not have one fellow in the backs who is not prepared to fight equally as hard to use it. A captain must have complete reliance on his pack leader. I never ever try to interfere. The only time I ever pass a comment to a pack leader is if I notice that one of the flankers is playing nasty little tricks when he is standing in the three-quarter line and that type of thing. I have always been very fortunate in playing with a pack leader who knows his job and gets the ball, and that is all we should ask. This can be worked out on the training field. The only thing I would say about forward play is that I think the two-handed catch in the lineout is a skill. I like the two handed catch because it stops the opposition backs racing up straight away in defence. A tap or anything else and the opposition can move up straight away. A catch makes them hesitate and that hesitation can give you three or four yards and that, to a three-quarter, is very important indeed.

Carwyn James: Before we go on to questions, I must say I was glad to hear Mike Gibson and John Dawes emphasising the business of taking the ball and giving it in one movement. That is the basis of any pattern and, as a coach, I find that this is the most difficult thing to teach young players. They come through to first-class level and they still cannot do it. It might take three months, it might take six months, it might take a year, it might take more, but you must get players to do that. Once they can do it then obviously the stage is set for the kind of pattern that we need in the British Isles, knowing the kind of players that we have had here for some years.

In New Zealand, they always play back to their strength in the pack, the scrum-half does it, the fly-half does it, with kicks back into the box. Their midfield players do it, or at any rate, they did. All their ploys, were geared to playing back to their forwards. Naturally, we tried to move the ball away from the All Blacks strength towards our own strength, I suppose.

Q. *Could you give details of the games you devised in practice to improve your handling?*

A. *Mike Gibson:* Basically, the training was done on the principle that if you want people to run a hundred yards, then they will do it more willingly when they have a ball in their hands than when you have them just monotonously running up and down a field.

So we had a simple transfer of a ball in forms of relay races. We would run ten yards, kick ahead, field that kick and run on to the edge of the 25 and then bring the ball back, doing the same thing.

Other times we would tune up by merely getting into circles and simply throwing the ball around with one man in the middle to distribute it each time. He would throw it through his legs or over his shoulder to maintain the surprise element and to develop dexterity.

We also grouped three players together and made them see how many passes they could get in running ten yards and back again.

We practised hard at passing the ball in front of the next

man. We had relay races between one team passing the ball and the other team running until we were quick enough to make the ball beat the man. Introduce an element of competition. It certainly sharpens people in that field of the game.

Another method we used was to train with two teams. The ball would be kicked to one team, who would then run it back either to the half-way line or to the far goal line, and the other side would simply set up in opposition. You have to have a referee - a person who would say that you would have been tackled in that situation or, if anybody makes a mistake, knocks it on or drops a pass, then it is their turn to kick the ball to the other team. I found that this was one of the great ways of training. You do an immense amount of work but you don't really appreciate it until you've finished.

Carwyn James: I was reading "Rugby News" from New Zealand, only about a couple of days ago and there was an article which said we never practised actually scoring a try in New Zealand. Well, you can devise a relay to do this. Your teams are each split into two groups, one behind the goal-line and one behind the 25. Throw the ball in front, then run at speed, pick it up and dive over the 25 line. The next guy picks it up, throws the ball, picks it up on the run and when he gets to the try line he dives over. These are little things but they relate to specific skills. Now there are two skills practised in this relay; picking the ball up on the run and actually scoring the try. We did this quite often. Willie John McBride almost did himself a nasty injury doing one of these belly-flops.

Alternatively, you can split players into groups of three and make them dive pass to each other. Believe me, it is pretty exhausting. If you vary it and put a ring of players and make them return the ball to a man in the middle who has to dive pass each time, he has to do about 30 belly-flops in quick succession. You get extremely fit if you do these. On a long tour, games of this sort are vitally important, because above anything else you must have variation in your training sessions. That is absolutely essential.

Ray McLoughlin has said that it is a good thing to change the pack leader. It is the same with the warming-up sessions. After the first fortnight or three weeks, I used to ask one of the players to take over the warming up. Then the warm-up was different, it was a different voice, they thought a bit about it and I think the players got far more out of it than if I had been doing the warm up all the time. I do this with my club at Llanelli as well. The players enjoy taking the sessions and certainly the other players value them enormously, because they don't know what is coming next.

Q. *How much emphasis would you put on backing up by flank forwards?*

A. In a word, essential. In these days it is difficult to get over the gain line, but if you do get there, the chances of scoring a try are still extremely small. You look for support, and this perhaps emphasises what John Taylor said about the question of open and blind side wing forwards. It does not matter too much which combination you use really. If the player is good enough he'll be there anyway. Continuity is the key word in the game these days, and if you look at the half-backs as the link between forwards and backs from set play, then surely the back row is the link with the backs from broken play. With our style of play, this is a situation which occurs a lot more than in the New Zealand style of play, where there is a greater concentration in setting up the ruck. I can distinctly remember two or three tries that we scored directly on that sort of basis. The one John Taylor scored against Otago from Gerald Davies' pass comes to mind. If you create an overlap or some situation whereby you get through the gain line, and there is no need to form a ruck, the very concentration of the wing forward in getting to that position sometimes means that all he has to do is run in.

Carwyn: Yes, I remember the try quite distinctly. It was fine work - good support.

Q. *Do you think the scrum-half should be the dictator of play, and also could you give us an idea of the relevance of the wing-threequarter in the modern game?*

A. *by John Dawes.* I was the substitute scrum-half in one game because Ray Hopkins had had a knock on the leg the game before and Gareth had a hamstring. Anyway, the fly-half was a certain Mr Gibson! We were in the changing room and "Chico" said: "Look, if I get another knock, I'll have to come off." At which Mike said very quickly, "We shall need two substitutes, then because I shall be off before him."

Which was rather hard, but realistic. Both our scrum—halves could create a gap and score a try and indeed they needed watching all the time. This, possibly more than the length of pass that Gareth had, was the reason why Barry was so successful. The opposition had first of all to worry about Gareth Edwards. As he has proved this year, in the Scottish game, he is a man that you have got to watch. If you have to concentrate on a scrum-half, really concentrate on him in defence, the fly-half has those extra few seconds and this is perhaps where we were very fortunate in New Zealand. We had two scrum-halves of that calibre. He must have the ability, of course, to size up the situation as it happens. He must be aware of lots of things. He must choose whether to get rid of the ball quickly, or do something on his own, he must know where his back row are. He is certainly a key man!

As far as wings were concerned, we were very fortunate in that we had one or two people who could really motor on the wings. Therefore, if we got the ball to them and put them into a one against one situation, maybe even a one against two situation, they could score tries. Certainly, our wings were the most gifted runners we had in the team, so it was our aim to get the ball to them as quickly as we could. And they repaid us in the work they did off the ball. This is something that perhaps you do not notice unless you are really serious about coaching. It was essential always, with John Williams as a full-back, to have someone covering him, and this was the job of the blind-side wing. So much so, in fact that if Carwyn ever advised a wing, it was to make sure that he knew where to go to be in a position to counter attack or to sweep up if anything went wrong.

The wing is not a prima donna these days. He is more than a runner-in of tries. He's there to work and work very hard.

I am sure that the biggest thing the wing must concentrate on is throwing the ball into the lineout. This is a skill which many people take for granted and it is not practised enough. Fortunately we did quite well in that respect in New Zealand.

Carwyn James: When John Taylor mentioned the difference in the style of play between Chris Laidlaw and Sid Going, he outlined many of the differences between our approach to scrum-half play and that in New Zealand, even though both Laidlaw and Going are All Blacks. Sid Going, with his low centre of gravity, is very difficult to stop, is always the alert type of scrum-half, he's always looking for a break. And because of this distinctive pattern in New Zealand you always expected him to make a break, to get over the gain line. You see, their idea is to reach the gain line as near to the set-piece as possible, therefore the scrum-half tries as hard as he can to do this and bring the back row into play.

Now "Chico" and Gareth played more of a waiting game. Mike talked about Barry John's powers to relax and to lull people into thinking that he was uninterested and what have you; well, I think that scrum-halves in our country can take the pressure off themselves by playing this kind of game, lulling the opposition into thinking that they are content just to pass the ball.

As far as the wings are concerned, it is my experience that they are very difficult people. They want to prove that they are very much faster than anyone else and you find them over-running too often and you find that their angle of running is wrong. This game is all about angles and unless their angle of take is right, then they are going to be in desperate trouble.

Mike was whispering in my ear just now, about a certain player in one of the tests in 1959. The try was on but the try was lost and the game was lost, simply because the stupid young man was in front of his centre. So you have them at that level, you have them right the way through. I always find wings very difficult to coach. It is very difficult to get inside their minds. They tend to over-run and to be over-anxious in both attack and in defence. I would say, nevertheless, that wing-three quarter play has changed probably more than any other position on the field.

Q. *Bearing in mind the usefulness of having an extra player in the back line for overlaps, why is it that in international rugby, it is common practice to use the wingers for throwing the ball in as opposed to, say, the hooker.*

A. *by Carwyn James*: All you want is the best thrower. It does not matter who he is. I felt that on tour the Lions' wings were all good throwers. They practised for hours and they did throw rather nicely. The main point there was that I did not want to operate with seven men in the line-out against New Zealand. We couldn't afford it. We had to have eight men for this con frontation. That was the underlying principle. Eight men - sometimes I wished we had nine! Certainly we couldn't afford to have seven. So the problem varies a great deal. In my club, the hooker throws in but on tour, against a pack like New Zealand, you certainly need eight men.

GOAL-KICKING: THE TORPEDO KICK

By *Bob Hiller*
(Harlequins and England)

I am glad I am going to appear in this book after all! Originally, I was supposed to be doing a joint thing with Barry John on "The Pressures on the Modern Player", but he jacked out on me. I think he found the pressure too much! Actually, what I think it was, he thought that talking with me would infringe his professional status... Anyway, I went to a lot of trouble to produce this visual aid slide entitled, "The King and I". I didn't bother with the music, but at least the slide has come in useful, because the King and I are going to do our best to describe the two different techniques of goalkicking - toe-kicking and instep kicking.

As you may have noticed, if you haven't fallen asleep by the time I get through all my preparations, I am a toe-kicker. Put like that, it sounds like a terrible confession. One of those things you read in the Sunday papers. Perhaps we should form a society called, "Toe-kickers Anonymous." Certainly, from the way the King went on in New Zealand, I felt as if I should have been the founder member. I don't know how he got so much power. He's three stone lighter than me, and yet he hit the ball such a crack you could hear the kick outside the ground. All the kids in New Zealand started kicking at goal with their insteps. They didn't want to know me and my toe. Ah well! That's show business.

Still, there was a time, about 200 years ago, when toe-kicking was all the thing, and I shall do my best to describe the technique before it becomes extinct. Or at any rate, before I become extinct!

I use two methods of kicking at goal:

(1) The torpedo kick.
(2) The upright kick.

I only use the upright kick in good conditions and from short range, say up to a maximum of 35 yards and within 15 yards on either side of the posts. If the range and the angle are any greater, I put the ball down flat and use the torpedo kick.

Let me deal with the torpedo kick first. That's the one that takes the stamina. It takes most of the words, too.

First of all, I turn with my back to the posts at the point where the kick has been awarded, and using the heel of my boot, I dig two holes side by side so that I make a hole in the turf twice as wide as my foot pointing towards the posts.

I then turn to face the posts and use my heel round the outside of the hole to kick back a ridge of divots in the shape of a horseshoe. I shape these with my hands so that they give me a tee about three inches high. As you can imagine, this does not make me too popular with groundsmen, but I have found that the better the tee, the better I kick. I kicked more consistently on the Lions tour of South Africa in 1968 than at any other time in my life, and it was simply because the grounds are so hard there that you cannot kick up a tee, so they bring on a bucket of earth or a bucket of sand and let you build a tee with it. I think this should be allowed in every country. It saves damage to the pitch and it saves so much time, too. I have been criticised for taking a long time over my kicks, but more than half the time I take is spent in building up the tee. Certainly, I think it would be better to allow earth or sand to be used rather than artificial tees because earth and sand are natural substances which can scatter into the ground. If you introduced plastic tees, you would have to introduce legislation, and I think that is unnecessary.

Once I have shaped the tee round the hole to my satisfaction, I look for the best end of the ball to kick. One end is always a bit rounder than the other, and that is the end I kick. If there is a valve and a lace, I always place those at the bottom and settle the ball on top of them. If there is no lace, I look for the straightest seam to place uppermost, though if you are playing with those thirty bob balls they use at Blackheath, you can look all day and you won't find a straight seam! I wonder Tony Jorden can kick any goals at all down there.

If the turf is fairly soft, I place the ball so that the end I am going to kick is above the hole and about one and a half inches above the lip of the tee. If the ground is hard, you have to bring the ball back more into the hole.

When I place the ball, I invariably aim it for the middle of the posts, even if there is a breeze. The more I kick, the more I come to the conclusion that a good kick well struck seldom deviates from its line. It's only if you get under the ball that it goes off line, or if you hit it thin. Obviously, I do most of my kicking at Twickenham, where you can't judge the wind anyway, so it is always safest to go for the middle of the posts. If there is a really high wind, I place the ball a bit flatter, but I never aim off outside the posts. One post or the other is the absolute limit.

I know I hit a big curve across the wind against Scotland at Murrayfield in 1968, but that was a lucky kick. I didn't hit it as I wanted to. I hit it thin, so that it flew low and wandered about. Fortunately, it wandered in the right direction, and the wind pulled it in. Had I hit the ball properly, though, it would have tumbled backwards through the air like a well hit golf ball and held its line. It is the back spin which holds it on line, and a kick which doesn't have back spin is not a good kick. Nine times out of ten, I aim for the middle of the posts.

When I use the torpedo kick, I take seven easy paces back from the ball. I find this gives me a four pace run-up. When I first started goalkicking, I found it very difficult to get in the right position. I used to go back too far and found myself stretching for the ball when I got to the kicking position. Now I consciously try to make my first step back a small one as I walk back from the ball.

I also make a conscious effort not to get too much to one side of the ball when I am lining myself up, otherwise I become over-conscious of having to use my hips through the ball. I position myself so that the centre of the posts, the ball and the middle of my feet are all in one line.

Then I settle myself down, and start my deep breathing routine. In any case, if I have been involved in a running move in the previous 20 minutes, I am out of breath and so I've got to get it back. At my age that takes time!

Ball teed up about three inches. Non-kicking foot placed short of the ball.

Impact position. The toe of the non-kicking foot is just short of the ball so that the kicking foot is swinging upwards as it makes contact.

I take a final look at the posts, and then look at the ball and I don't take my eye off the ball from then on. I concentrate on a spot about three inches from the end I am going to kick, because that is how far my boot will bury itself in the ball at impact. I don't look at the end of the ball. I concentrate on the ball and I take these three deep breaths. That is when the crowd usually starts booing. I must admit that if they don't boo, I have a tendency to think that I have not taken long enough over my preparations! Booing doesn't put me off, though. The players on the other side often try to distract me, too, but that doesn't bother me either. They try to move about and catch my attention. But after I've started concentrating on the ball, I don't notice them. Sometimes, I will see someone like Derek Quinnell moving to one side and leaning sideways like the Tower of Pisa to try to put me off when I am placing the ball, but I tell him to move across a bit and we both have a laugh. I never see him once I settle down.

The jack-knife position of the follow-through.

The three pace kick with the ball upright. This goal gave Bob Hiller 100 points on tour in Australia and New Zealand.

The Waterloo hooker is a great lad for this sort of thing, too. He starts talking. He says, "He's easily put off." The last time we played them, he said that when I took a kick. As soon as I hit it, I knew it was going over. It went about a foot to one side of the middle of the posts. I said, "You put me off a bit that time. I usually put it straight through the middle."

Actually, as a bit of a humorist myself, I am disappointed with the remarks of the different crowds. After all, it is a classic opportunity for slapstick, isn't it? There is all this mumbo-jumbo of preparation and the deep breathing bit, and the quiet. It's the genuine banana skin situation. But no one says anything original.

I remember once we were playing in Newport for the Harlequins, and it had rained so much in the morning that there was about two inches of water on the pitch. The ball was practically floating. We had a penalty kick early in the game somewhere near the halfway line and I decided to have a go. Just as I was getting ready to kick, I heard Joe McPartlin say, "If this goes over, I'm going to write to the Pope and tell him it's a miracle." It never left the ground.

As I say, my seven steps back give me a four pace run-up to kick the ball. I put my non-kicking foot down a bit short of the ball, because I want to kick the ball on the up. George Cole does the same thing. His non-kicking foot is even further behind the ball than mine. I remember I was having a bit of trouble with my kicking when I was at Oxford, and Vivian Jenkins spent an afternoon with me and he said that he thought I was putting my non-kicking foot down too close to the ball. That is what the purists say you should do, but as soon as I put my non-kicking foot down a few inches short, I started to hit the ball really well again.

By coming into the ball square, and not consciously using my right hip, I have to jack knife my body and throw my arms forward to provide the right balancing reaction to my kick. I don't do this consciously, but it is clear from all the photographs of me that I do it, and I realise that it has to be, because if for any reason my head goes back, I lose all my power. I have drawn some match-stick men to show you what position I am in when I kick, and what position I try to avoid because I know it is not good.

The body position to achieve.   The body position to avoid.

If you come too close to the ball with your non-kicking foot, you either hit down on the ball or hit it with your boot travelling parallel to the ground instead of hitting it on the up so that your boot is travelling in the same plane as the ball. This is one of the secrets of length and the other is the follow-through.

I used to jab-kick the ball, but now I concentrate on a good follow-through with the kicking leg. It helps to get the right direction and it adds power. Of course, I am 6ft 2in and I weigh more than 14 stones so I have the length of leg and the weight of leg to kick this way. I don't need to use my hips to get more power, though I must admit that I found goalkicking much more difficult when I started playing first-class Rugby and I weighed only 12½ stones. Now I find I foul up my kicking if I try to get my hips into it.

When I want to get more length on a kick, I swing my kicking leg just a bit quicker, but I don't change anything else.

I am very fussy about my boots and socks. I always wear two pairs of socks, with foam rubber insoles, and I always wear boots with a half-square toe-cap. I roughen the end with a file and never polish it. I always wear boots the same size and I lace them up as tight as I can so that they almost hurt. It may be psychological, but I find it is very off-putting if my foot moves around inside the boot.

A lot of what I have said may not apply to another kicker. It is up to the individual to experiment with the variables to find the combination which suits him best, but five rules always apply.

(1) You MUST tee up the ball properly.

(2) You MUST be lined up properly.

(3) You MUST keep looking at the ball.

(4) You MUST swing straight.

(5) You MUST follow through straight.

Having said all that about the torpedo kick, it will come as a relief to you to know that I can say all I want to say about the upright kick in about four paragraphs.

You do not need to build a tee to place the ball upright. You just kick the smallest possible hole in the ground and stand the ball in it so that the vertical plane is aiming for the middle of the posts.

As I have said, I do not attempt to kick further than 35 yards with this kick, and I never use it for wide-angled kicks.

For this kick, I use a three pace run-up, stepping back from the ball with my left foot. (I don't know why, but when I step back from the ball with the torpedo kick, I step back with my right foot first.)

When I move into this kick, I still put my non-kicking foot down short of the ball, and I tend to get my body over the ball a bit more. Otherwise, all the other rules apply.

Once you have established a drill, stick to it. Everyone misses kicks, just as a golfer misses putts.

This is the one thing that experience of top-class rugby has taught me. I used to panic and go to pieces if I missed four kicks in succession. Now I don't. I know that the chances are that the next four will go over.

GOAL-KiCKiNG: THE iNSTEP KiCK

*By **Barry John***

(Cardiff and Wales)

Goalkicking is concerned with two things; accuracy and distance. It is not a bit of good being the most accurate goalkicker in the world if you can only kick the ball 25 yards, and this is the problem which faces someone with my physique. I have never weighed much more than 11 stones, so the only way I can get the power to kick goals from 45 yards is to make use of the suppleness in my body and the flexibility in my hips to unwind from the ball and wind back through it with a big hip turn and a big backswing of my kicking leg.

You just cannot do this when you use a torpedo kick, because to kick with your toe, you have to keep your shoulders more or less square on to the ball. Accordingly, I go round the corner, as they say, and kick the ball with my instep, which as you know, is the top of my foot. Even then, 45 yards is about my limit.

When I was at Gwendraeth Grammar School, I twice scored more than 100 points in a season by placing the ball upright and kicking it with my toe. I have to confess I thought it was all a bit unsporting because I was using a pair of thirty bob boots from the local Co-op which had such a huge great flat slab across the toe that I couldn't miss!

I wear a soft-toed boot now, but sometimes I still kick with my toe just for the fun of it. In one or two games in my last season, I kicked goals with my instep, and then with my toe with the ball upright and finally with the ball laid flat for a torpedo kick. I had to kick those with my toe as well, of course, and to do it, I curled my toes back inside my soft boot and kicked the ball off the quarter of an inch of leather on the end of the sole.

"Put THAT in your pipe and smoke it," I thought, but I have to admit that those sort of carryings-on would never do for Bob Hiller! Better by half use my thirty bob Co-op boots.

The funny thing is that I was never first-choice goalkicker for anyone in between the time I was at Gwendraeth Grammar School and when I went on the 1971 Lions tour of New Zealand. At Cardiff, in the year before the Lions went to New Zealand, I was fourth choice behind Robin Williams, Dennis Gethin and Gareth Edwards, and I remember in the game against Swansea, I tried to convert a try from halfway out with my toe and did not even reach the crossbar. They showed that on television when they did the "This Is Your Life" programme on me! I covered my face with my hands.

John Dawes has said that it was the kick I put over against New South Wales at Sydney at the beginning of the tour that convinced him that I had the power to become the Lions' goalkicker in the tests. I am glad he mentioned that, because it was pouring with rain and the kick was from out of the mud on the cricket square in the middle of the field. I did not realise he wanted me to kick for touch instead of for goal but he let me get on with it, and as far as I am concerned, that was the kick of the tour, because it was out of the wet.

I often wonder how things would have gone in New Zealand if the Lions had not been so lucky with the weather. While we were there, they had their best winter for years and years, and I know how much difference that made to my style of goal-kicking. When we got on a wet pitch in the second test at Christchurch, I began to be conscious of losing my foothold on my run-up almost for the first time on tour. It was the last time, too, because the good weather came back. I could never have kicked as well as Bob Hiller did on that splashy pitch at Greymouth. In fact, I must say that I think that if it had been as wet as it normally is in a New Zealand winter, Bob would have come out on top.

Fortunately for me, though, the grounds were nearly always dry and the only problem I had was when the sun got in my eyes! That actually happened once against Southland. The sun was streaming straight between the posts and I just could not sight

Head down, body leaning backwards, right hip well forward and kicking foot angled on a step diagonal down and across the ball. The ball is placed with the lace facing the posts.

them properly. I think it was the only kick I missed that day. But fancy having problems with the sun in Invercargill! The only things that have ever bothered other Lions teams have been the rain and the snow.

As I say, good ground conditions are a great asset to an instep goal-kicker, and if he has them, he can complete his kick at goal in only a fraction of the time taken by a really conscientious torpedo kicker. For instance, it only takes me ten or fifteen seconds to take a kick at goal, even in an international match, and because I do it as quickly as that, people get the impression that I am being nonchalant about the whole thing. Nothing could be further from the truth. Those ten or fifteen seconds are full of concentration.

It is the same with everything I do on the rugby field. I may give the impression of being so relaxed that I am almost casual about it but believe me, succeeding in what I am doing matters very much to my pride as a rugby player. I don't mind other teams thinking, "Oh, he looks as if he could do it in his sleep," because that gives me a psychological advantage. I know different. I know just how much I am concentrating.

When I pick the ball up to take the kick, for instance, I examine it just as carefully as Bob Hiller does. Like him, I put the valve and the lace on the far side of the ball when I place it for the kick, and like him, I look to see which is the more comfortable end to kick. Obviously, when I am kicking the ball with the top of my foot I am not going to bury my toe in the point of the ball as I would for a torpedo kick, but to an instep kicker, one part of the ball usually looks more comfortable to kick than another, and that is the part I choose.

I place the ball upright for the kick, and so I only need to make a little squiggle in the ground with my heel so that the ball will stand in it. If anything I stand the ball so that the top is leaning slightly back towards me.

In placing the ball, I pick out a flight path to the centre of the posts. I know from experience that from the middle of the field and to the left of the posts, a well hit kick of mine will curve slightly to the left in the air. This is the natural flight for an instep kicker. I run up to the ball on a slight curve from the left and I kick the ball with my right foot pointing down and across the ball on a diagonal. This brings my kicking leg round on the same line as my run-up and gives the ball its gently curving flight to the left.

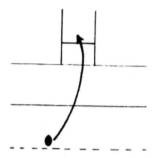

Pick out a flight path to the centre of the posts…

When the kick is from an acute angle to the right of the posts, I change my technique because this curving flight reduces the width between the posts even more and makes it even harder to kick the goal. Therefore, I hit the ball more in the middle, instead of slightly to the right of the vertical centre line and I push my kicking leg straight through so that I can hold the ball up on a straighter flight, but I will come back to that later.

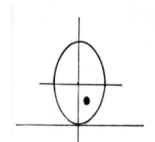

The impact position for the normal instep kick.

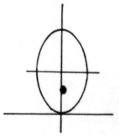

The impact position for the instep kick which reduces the curve of the ball to the left in its flight and which pushes the ball through on a straighter line.

As I say, I imagine the flight path of the kick when I place the ball. If, for example, I am 40 yards from the posts in fairly settled wind conditions and I am in the middle of the field, I aim the ball for a spot about four feet inside the right post. Then I know that if I strike the ball well, it will curve in so that it goes through the middle.

If, on the other hand, I am on the left hand side of the field, I aim the ball for the far post. I only aim outside the post if there is a wind. Bob is right when he says that the wind does not have much effect on a really well struck torpedo kick, but it does have a bigger effect on an instep kick.

If the kick is from the right hand side of the field, I aim the ball just inside the near post and straighten my kick. If the angle is even wider and I need a lot of power, I aim the ball a couple of yards outside the near post. After all, you must remember that when a try is scored in the corner, a conversion kick from the 25 yard line has to travel about 42 yards and at that range I am pretty near my maximum power.

I straightened the kick well when I converted Gerald's try from the right touchline in the third Test at Wellington, but the best kick I ever hit from the right hand side of the field was against Auckland. It started to curve to the left and then went back again. I don't know what happened but the papers said it looked as if the ball was on a string. I wish I knew how I did it!

Having placed the ball, I stand up with a little jump to relax myself, and take four easy paces back to give me a three pace run-up. The first step is a small one and the others are comfortable. I walk back on a continuation of the same gentle curve of the flight path. I might then just shuffle an inch or two to get myself into exactly the right position. When I see some of these round the corner kickers taking huge steps sideways, I know they are going to be erratic because it is so unnatural, and the whole essence of kicking is to be natural.

Once I have got back into position, I relax. Sometimes I think of some stupid things when I stand in front of a kick. I flick my hands and make sure I can feel my fingernails. Then I know I'm relaxed. I'm in charge of myself.

When I run up to the ball, I concentrate on my non-kicking foot. That's the important one to me, and like Bob Hiller, I don't put it anyway near as close as most of the coaching manuals say you should. I put it down really quite a long way short of the ball, almost as much as six inches, and it is not straight, either. It is bent in to the ball at an angle.

This helps me to clear my hips through the ball and give me the backswing so that I can hit it with a real whoomph. I don't think about this consciously, because as I say, the essence of my style of kicking is relaxation and naturalness and control. In one sense, I try to caress the ball with my instep but in another, I know I have got to kick it well. All kicks have to be kicked well, even the little short chips. If you try to baby them, you will miss them.

A little chip kick to convert the try Barry John scored himself in the third Test at Wellington.

When I get back to about 40 yards from the posts, I have to be more aggressive in my run-up. I know I've really got to start stamping my feet...

The other thing that looks odd about my goalkicking is that I am leaning back from the ball as I hit it. Perhaps it is because by putting my non-kicking foot down short of the ball, I have to lean back to hit the ball on the up. Perhaps it is a natural compensation for the length of my backswing and the movement of my hips.

When I kick the ball, I aim to hit it with the flat part of my foot just behind and to the right of my big toe and I aim to hit the ball about two thirds of the way down and on a spot just to the right of the vertical centre line. If you quarter the ball with two imaginary lines, my impact point is in the bottom right hand quarter and just to the right of the vertical centre line.

The longer the kick, the longer my backswing. When I get back to about 40 yards from the posts, I have to be more aggressive in my run-up. I know I've really got to start stamping my feet. At the same time, I know I must not lose my control. I did that in the first test against New Zealand at Dunedin. The result was that I topped the kick. So I try to reproduce this feeling of relaxed aggression.

The easy follow-through position across the ball after a little chip of a conversion from near the posts.

For somebody of my build, a 40 yarder needs a bit of everything. With the short ones, I need only take one pace and chip the ball up with my foot more across the ball. The action is almost languid. With the long ones, though, I need this aggression. My foot is pointing down the ball at an angle nearer the vertical, and it follows through a long way. I don't think about the follow through, but it is the inevitable consequence of the longer backswing and the bigger hip action.

With those kicks on the right side of the field and at an acute angle, I hit the ball on the vertical line down through the centre, rather than to the right, but of course, I still hit it in the bottom half. With this kick, the heel of my non-kicking foot is more open, and I push my kicking leg straight through instead of letting it come round. I look at the ball a long time, too, but of course I do that on all my kicks. You don't need to look to see where the ball is going. The crowd will tell you. Anyway, you know from the feel of the kick.

There is a tremendous satisfaction in kicking well. I think about words like "thump" and "whoomph", so obviously it is not only the finesse but the power which gives me that satisfaction. It's a marvellous feeling.

Two of the best kicks I ever hit were against France in Cardiff this year. They were struck so well that I didn't bother to watch them all the way. I just ran back. I thought, "Nothing will stop those, boy."

COACHING THE 1971 BRITISH LIONS

By *Carwyn James*
(Llanelli and Wales)

We have had an excellent technical analysis from the forwards and we have considered the approach and attitude to the game. Now it is also necessary to know your opponents. There are two sides to this game - by far the most important one is how you play the game yourself, but an appreciation of the opponents themselves does have some significance. Going to another country, obviously one tried to get to know the people and I feel that the New Zealander, because of his environment and the nature of his country, is somewhat different from the kind of animal we breed here. Neville Cardus has written very nicely about this. I recall reading an article by him which was called "Cricket without Art" and he writes about the make-up of the Australian. There is a will to win in everything he does. Trumper plays an elegant shot, but it was meant to kill. Then in the same article he talks about May and Cowdrey coming to the wicket. Cardus says, "There wasn't anything which savoured of ill breeding or bad manners. There was a suggestion of modesty about everything that happened," and then when the shots were played, he says, "There was grace and there was charm."

The same difference is apparent to the visitor in the game of rugby. In a country like New Zealand the stress is always on the physical side of the game. They love it. They love the perspiration, and I had a feeling that they were not all that impressed by the inspiration. And to a certain extent, I think that sums up the personalities of the two peoples coming into conflict on a Rugby field. The Lions backs that New Zealand put on a pedestal were John Williams, John Bevan and Michael Gibson, people whom they admired enormously for their hard tackling and for bringing this physical thing into the game.

Gerald Davies? Oh yes. Not a bad player. The King? He was never really understood. He was a being from another planet.

That try, I shall never forget it, against New Zealand Universities - and incidentally New Zealand Universities played the kind of game that I like seeing. There was a scrummage on their 25. The ball came out to Barry. He moved the top half of his body right, without moving his feet at all, and one or two back-row forwards went the wrong way. Then he moved left, right, left and under the sticks. Poetry! Some of the boys have mentioned that I have said that you can play at a conscious level. The coach can take players to the conscious level. You could not go along with Barry John on a try like that. That was sheer poetry! Ray McLoughlin called it the unconscious! I do not know what it is. It is certainly above the conscious level anyway. This is flair, this is imagination, this is genius! The kind of thing that people have knocked us about for years, particularly when coaching first became a reasonably fashionable word. It was said, "You will coach flair and imagination out of your good players." As Ray Williams said, and he has often been quoted, "I don't believe in bad coaching either." That I think is the important thing.

That try by the King was received with a bit of a hush by the New Zealand spectators, not because of bad sportsmanship, but because it was not their line of country. In their pattern, Barry's opposite number would kick the ball high into the box, or kick a high up and under and the spectators would be on the edge of their seats, loving it, enjoying it! This was rugby football! Put the ball in the air, let's have eight men going after this ball and let us feel the thump! That is rugby!

From six years of age, or seven, or eight, they played the same pattern, completely rigid and predictable. Of course this produced winning rugby. Why should they change?

Well, let us have a fairly close look at this pattern and then talk about counters. On the training field in New Zealand teams work terribly hard. They run and they run, and there is no ball near the place. This makes them much better runners round the paddock. The sweat pours off. They work hard but they are not learning skills. Possibly, I am having my own back a little by saying this because those New Zealanders who came and watched our training sessions early on had a bit of a giggle.

We'd start off a session with a warm-up, a gentle warm-up. We would run around, do a few press-ups, a few exercises to get our muscles working. We would have a bit of a chat before we got down to the serious stuff. Then we'd do a few skills in the round. Players would be lined up in six groups of 5 shall we say, and they would take off in sprints, looping outside each other, to complete rounds of passing. Then the same groups would run a 60 yard circle with the leading man running 10 yards and putting the ball down for the next man to pick up while running full tilt and then do the same thing and so on. We introduced as many skills as possible while doing this combination of ball work and running. This meant that the training was getting tougher. The players were running 70 or 80 yards each time and having done this on about six or seven occasions, they were looking forward to what was coming next.

There had to be a period of relaxation of some kind, something not as intense, and I found that it was most useful then to have a period of a quarter of an hour or 20 minutes where individual skills could be practised. For instance, have three wings in a line throwing, as if they were throwing to touch. The other wing placed as a full back, so that you had the beginnings of a counter attack. We would put the front rows together and let them get on with the weight lifting, to prepare for the scrummaging session later. We had the lock forwards jumping, working very close together in that part of the field where they could easily be joined by the half backs. Meanwhile, the six back row forwards would go into a corner and work out their moves. They were told that later we should call for a few, so they should have them worked out. This was a period when people could look at their own game. Then gradually you could bring the props and the locks together, and eventually bring the back row to them, so that you had a complete scrum. In other words, we started with an individual skill session of, say, 20 minutes, and developed it gradually into a unit skill session.

"Lots of their skills have to be practised standing still. Quick movement of the ball…" David Duckham, John Dawes, Gareth Edwards, Arthur Lewis, John Williams, Gerald Davies and Barry John fire the ball to Mike Gibson in the middle.

We practised scrummaging on the Monday and the Thursday, two days away from the game, because this was the hard stuff and one did, say 30, 40, 50 scrummages in the context of the game, not in the same place on the field. We would say, "Right, we'll do five this time. That pack will go into a locking position, the other pack will shove on each put-in." We would work from one end of the field to the other. Each time the two eights would go down together. That is important. A number of little points are consistent each time or else I would blow the whistle and make them get up and start again. Each time, the forwards had to run from one scrum to the next, for half an hour, forty minutes, perhaps an hour, sometimes more.

During this time, Doug Smith and John Dawes would be doing a lot of these ball games that I mentioned earlier, because I find that one of the difficulties in a training session is that while you can easily employ forwards for about forty minutes or fifty minutes or whatever it is, it is hard to keep the backs going for a similar period. Their skills mean running, but they cannot be running for forty or fifty minutes. So lots of their skills have to be practised standing still. Quick movement of the ball.

The next session would be semi-opposed. I want to emphasise that I don't believe in unopposed rugby practice because it

If they did 20 or 30 of these belly flops, it meant quite a lot of work…

becomes terribly artificial, as Ray McLoughlin mentioned yesterday. You have got to have at least another pack in opposition. Then you have so many options open to you. I don't care so much about putting pressure on the backs. You want the backs to display, to build their confidence and to reveal that they can pass at speed. Usually, when you put pressure on them by having a chap in the middle of the field, he just messes them up too much. Other people will say that, well, it is important that backs should also have pressure put on them. Well, fair enough, I think that the back row of the opposition can try to do that.

In New Zealand, their practice was always unopposed, to my knowledge. And it is artificial. It is not geared to the game situation. With another pack you can have line-outs, you can have scrummaging, and that is important. Then, after about twenty minutes or half an hour of that semi-opposed practise, we would finish off with sprinting and then a bit of weight lifting.

In the early days of the tour, training usually lasted for two hours. Eventually that was condensed to about an hour and a half, and I felt that it was a better training session as a result.

That, then, was the kind of session that we had. The New Zealanders felt that it was all too gentle, that there was far too much variation in it. This came by implication, of course. I seem to recall that down in Wanganui for instance, we had a training session there and the locals were not terribly impressed, and then the local side had a training session a couple of hours after, and they really worked hard apparently, running, running, running, and they all thought that it was a most impressive session. It depends on how you look at them. It comes back to the point, of the physical nature of the game where people very often are unthinking and, are also unsmiling. Now, I don't think it is a compliment that somebody has written a book called *The Unsmiling Giants*. I think it is important to see the game in perspective. John Williams said once that there should always be a moment in the game when a person can smile at something. We had this impression of unsmiling giants, a machine, geared to play a certain way. That was why I felt it was so important for our boys to be thinking at all times. You've got to out-think the opposition. You've got to think for yourself - not because you've done it 999 times before, but when the next occasion comes you've got to think about what you are doing.

As Doug Smith so rightly says, there are many good forwards in New Zealand. It is a question of environment. So many of them are farmers, who live very close to the soil, and they are tough. They make it their duty to be tough.

We used to have our coal miners, steel workers and so on, but we have them no longer. If you look at the Welsh team or any other British team these days, you'll find their toughness comes from weight training in the gymnasium. Usually they are men, not really as tough - I'm not talking about strength now - but naturally tough as some of these men are. There are plenty of that breed in New Zealand - the Keith Murdochs, the Colin Meads - hard, rugged men. All corners. They've still got them. Now I admire them for the way they work in unison, for their close support work, shoulder down the line, close inter-passing. I remember Rhys Williams telling me, after he came back from the Lions tour of 1959. He said, "That pack, they work so closely together, if you threw a blanket you'd find seven or eight forwards underneath it.

And when they are going forward, wave after wave of them, from one ruck situation to another, it is a frightening sight. At least it is from the stand. I don't know what it is like from the field, but from the stand it is certainly frightening. Now this is ingrained in New Zealand packs. It has been drilled from an early age and they do it very well.

I think that possibly the seeds of the All Blacks' failure in 1971 were sown in 1967 under Freddie Allen. They tasted the delights of the French forward running game and they had the players who could do it. This led to their play becoming a bit looser and this is their fear at the moment. This is why I feel that Bob Duff will get the job of coach when they come here next season. They will want to tighten up their game. I read an article about their final trial recently, before they went on their internal tour. They talked about Alan Sutherland being a great forward in the loose but they implied that possibly he was not doing the hard stuff, the donkey work if you like, which really is expected of a New Zealand forward.

We were very fortunate that the All Blacks played Brian Lochore and Colin Meads as lock forwards, players who were neither lock forwards nor No. 8's really, a sort of betwixt and between, with the result that the play was much looser than one would expect of a New Zealand pack. This looseness has crept in because the All Blacks put such an emphasis on the running side of the game. Well, obviously, the first duty of the front five is to do the basics well, the scrummaging, the line-out work, and so on, and obviously, in the context of the New Zealand game, the rucking, at which, of course, they are quite supreme. But the tight play, the hard graft must be done. Forwards must not fringe, but there was a tendency with some of the players I have mentioned, to fringe too much and not really get to the thick of things. This is a danger we must all beware. Its all right to say of a player, "Oh, he's marvellous in the loose, he runs well, he's a handler, he's a high-stepper, he's everything." But is he doing his work in the tight? It all starts there. The first function of a forward is to win possession.

Well, let's look very briefly at the immediate issues. I will not go into the technicalities of forward play, because that has been done already. However I must say that I was surprised, very surprised that Ivan Vodanovich when he sent his epistle out from on high to the New Zealand coaches during the season just before we came, did not mention anything at all about scrummaging. He did not tell his coaches that the standard of scrummaging in New Zealand was bad. He mentioned other things in his epistle but nothing at all about scrummaging. Now I would have thought that since they had come back defeated from South Africa where, you know, the gospel according to Danie Craven has to be a lot of hard scrummaging work, that Ivan would have seen the weakness exposed and consequently laid a great deal of stress on this. However, we discovered very early in the tour that their scrummaging was not of the high quality that we expected. As Ian and Ray have said, too often there were players who had been converted into props, a very specialist job. We did the very same thing in one or two matches but we learned our lesson and it was not done out of choice. I did the same thing this year with the Llanelli team in the Final of the Welsh Cup and played a lock forward at tight head and Neath shoved us all round the park. It doesn't usually work out. The apprenticeship of being a prop takes rather a long period of time.

Well, the scrummaging work in New Zealand was not all that good and I would say to everybody preparing a side for the incoming All Blacks to place a great deal of emphasis on good hard scrummaging and when you pick your forwards, think in terms of good prop forwards. You must have them, good scrummagers, and make absolutely certain that your flankers are prepared to shove.

As far as the details are concerned, discuss them with the players involved. For example, the tightness of a scrum so that the shove is transmitted as one unit. That is the important thing. Every single person in the pack must make his contribution and no one must ease up for the whole eighty minutes.

I remember seeing England playing against Australia in 1966-67 and thinking what a marvellous shove they had in the first two scrums. After that, it disappeared. I don't know whether the pack leader forgot about it or what but it was very good when he started and it should have been kept up for eighty minutes. This is the only area in the game when you are in direct physical confrontation with your opponents and psychologically for every member of the side there is nothing better than to see the opposing pack in retreat. As a fly half anyway, I always felt from that first scrummage that I knew whether it was going to be an interesting day or not, whether I was going to be on my toes or on my heels. The waves were transmitted from that very first scrummage. The backs derive a tremendous psychological advantage when they see that their forwards have the beating of their opponents in the scrummage.

Now what about the line-out? So far, possibly, we have discussed too much of the negative side of it, the retaliation side, the compression side, and not really so much about trying to play within the law as we know it. I would like to say, therefore, that the Lions did practise the moves that we would do in this country where we try to play within the law. I try not to coach outside the law and at Llanelli usually I ask a referee to come along and watch the training session and if one tries a ploy or tries a move one wants to know whether it is acceptable to the referee. I think that is important.

We know that the line-out is a complete and utter shambles, but we did try to create. Obviously we worked the peel at the back of the line. "Sandy" Carmichael was particularly good at this and I recall him scoring at Wellington. Towards the end of tour, we moved away from the peel at the back of the line to the peel round the front. We wanted more playing area to extend the All Blacks even further and therefore it was a good thing to suck them into the narrow side of the field. We would throw, say to Willie John at two and then "Mighty Mouse" at four, would come round the front and take it from Willie John. Ian was so small anyway that they couldn't see him coming round the front. Ian would go over the gain line as far as he possibly could, then he would make his contact with the opposition. By this time he would have support who would climb over him and the ball would be thrust back.

You then had the opposition near the touch line, you would suck the pack back to the side of the field and then with Gareth's long pass our backs had plenty of room. We would take the opposition to one side and move it across to the other side. So there was a certain amount of creativity as far as we were concerned even in the line-out, despite the fact that the line-out is a shambles - and let's get this perfectly straight - it is not only a shambles in New Zealand. It is a shambles in this country as well and we've got to put this right pretty soon. I know that schoolmasters might have been unhappy to hear us talking about compression and retaliation but again may I say that we just had to do it.

I shall never forget that first meeting that Doug and I attended with the New Zealand Council and members of the Referees Association and one referee who happened to be John Pring. After we had asked a few questions about the scrummage to break the ice, (I wasn't really concerned about the scrummage, because after the refereeing of Kevin Crowe and Craig Ferguson in Australia I knew that we were on a very good wicket as far as scrums were concerned in New Zealand) - I said, "What about the space between the lines of forwards?" One gentleman said, "Oh, between four and five inches," so I thought, "Dear me, yes."

"Oh no," says somebody else, "you're wrong, between eight and nine inches," and so it went on. I think we eventually finished up between twelve and fourteen inches. Well it didn't matter. It was just an introductory question. I said, "Now what happens? You throw the ball into the space, so players must move into it to take the ball." "Yes, of course," they said. "How many of them?" I asked knowing full well, of course, that what has been happening in New Zealand for donkeys years has been that the whole line has moved across, and therefore creating a new gain line if you allow them. This is to be seen on film of the '63 and the '67 All Blacks. It is there for everybody to see. Their first reaction when the ball is thrown is that they come across in a solid wall.

In answer to my question, one gentleman said, "Inevitably, there must be some compression." I can see him now. I said, "Thank you very much." End of discussion. Moved on to another point hurriedly. Went back and saw the boys in the hotel the following morning at half past nine. I said, "Boys you are going out this morning and you are going to compress like hell. We will compress for an hour, and we did compress for an hour. When that ball was thrown in, the two lines came together with a fearful clatter. It was a bit dangerous but nobody was killed and Terry

McLean in the "Auckland Herald" next morning said that he had never seen such a session in his life; it was so obvious that the Lions were taking the mickey out of New Zealand line-out play. Terry should have known better because by implication he inferred that this would only happen in a training session; it wouldn't happen in a match. But of course it had to happen in a match and the referee had to sort it out for himself.

You see in New Zealand in the last few years, you just cannot think of a great jumper. The Delme Thomases of this world do not exist there because jumping is not possible.

This was quite apparent in the All Blacks' final trial before we arrived. Doug Smith and I appeared on television in the first week and they showed us film of the final trial. The match was a bit rough. I don't know whether they were trying to impress us. Anyway, we were asked questions: "Well, what do you think of that? Hard stuff isn't it?"

"Oh no, it is pretty gentle you know, pretty gentle," we said.

But Peter Whiting took a fearful hammering in that trial. He was a new man coming through. It is very, very difficult for a young forward to break through into the top class in New Zealand. The Meads of this world see that they are put through the mill and Whiting took a hell of a hammering in that final trial but to his credit he made it and he is a good forward. But because of the way that they play in the line-out it is rare for anybody to develop into a great line-out jumper. Roy John or Delme Thomas or people of that kind were and are really good two handed jumpers and the game needs them.

Now what will happen eventually I don't know. I think possibly we may see the reintroduction of blocking as we had it in the early fifties. This might solve a few of the problems. At the moment, there is this tremendous gulf between the text book and reality. In the book, a chap jumps and people bind very nicely on either side of him. It looks very good. He holds the ball and back it comes. Well, what happens in New Zealand is that when, say, number five goes for the ball - and they are all potential line-out ball getters, they work on this premise - you will find that six and four will isolate him completely. They don't bind on him. They bind on the opposition. In other words, blocking goes on.

Well, it may be a good thing to reintroduce blocking into the game and make it legal and make lifting legal. The point is that they are not legal at the moment.

It is not that we did not want to create, not that we did not want to play within the law, not that we wanted to get our retaliation in first. It is simply that we would not have lived in New Zealand unless we did those things. We had to do it. This is the way that they play the game in New Zealand. There has to be this physical confrontation. There is a mental wearing down if you allow it.

By batting the ball on two-handed like this and saving the split-seconds which he would have taken to catch and pass the ball, John Williams…

Now let's move to the ruck. There, the All Blacks are the masters. This is their creative contribution to world rugby. South Africa may be equally good at the maul but New Zealand have been excellent at the ruck. It is their brain child and they love it and they will create all manner of situations in order to have a ruck. As somebody said, New Zealand teams often give the impression that it is much nicer to create the ruck than score the try.

A week or so after the Lions came back I received a paper from New Zealand and the headline was "We was conned". The story went on to say how the Lions' management - this is Doug Smith not me - kept on saying that the All Blacks were overplaying their hand as far as the ruck was concerned. Now we believed this. The ruck of course is important and the maul is important in the modern game but not to the extent possibly that they played it in New Zealand. Some of us are old enough to remember that after a tackle one had to play the ball with the foot. Then they changed the law. These days after a tackle you can pick the ball up, and move it. There is more continuity in the game. I don't think New Zealand likes that law you know. I am not absolutely certain that they all realise that this change has occurred, but the whole point is that the change has reduced the number of rucks in a game. What a nuisance from a line-out to have twenty yards between the opposing backs - makes it a bit of a sissy game, you see. How can you possibly create a ruck from a line-out when people are twenty yards away from each other? Who the hell was our member on the International Board when this happened? He must have been slipping! Thank God for the scrum because from the scrum we can work back to our strength, we can create the ruck from the scrum. We can wheel those devils a little bit away from the open side, we'll exert a bit of pressure, play tight outside and then we'll be there bit nearer to the point of breakdown, and that big second five-eighth we've got will crash and he will take the tackle.

...made a try for David Duckham against North Auckland like this.

How did Johann Claassens counter that? Well, Claassens said - he must have thought in terms of the scrummage, because that was our counter - "We won't let the buggers wheel. We'll disrupt their scrum. That's a start." He then got hold of "Joggie" Jansen and told him, "Now look, when that ball comes out from the scrum you've got to be over that gain line and you've got to hit your man so hard that he does not want to come again, or again, or again. Then Ellis and Greyling will pick up the loose ball." So it was Jansen, not MacRae who appeared in the headlines. It was a fine, marvellous counter.

But you cannot do that on tour. You cannot allow one of the midfield players to be crash tackling like mad in every game against second five-eighths. You would need quite a supply of players if you were going to do that. So obviously as far as we were concerned, the counter was the other thing, in the scrummage to give them bad ball. But I must confess, that we did not see a great deal of the MacRae ploy on the last tour.

Thirdly, and this is another reason why the number of rucks are minimised, the game is far more open than it ever was and it does allow players, particularly full backs, to attack and to counter-attack. The game is more fluid, and this again has cut the number of rucks that you have in a game. Now some people in New Zealand did not really believe this. This man in the newspaper said, "Let us get back to our rucking game. This is our strength. We were conned by the Lions' management."

I hope they do it but I doubt it. The game in 1972 is vastly different from what it was in 1967. The game is changing - it's a different game now and there is evidence I think that the penny has dropped in New Zealand. Some of the journalists were quick to point this out; Bob Howitt, Editor of "Rugby News" for instance, wrote to me pretty soon after Lions tour saying, "You caned Wellington and then they went through the provinces of New Zealand winning all their matches. And they did it playing Lions rugby." It does not matter what kind of rugby you call it. What is significant is that there must come a realisation sooner or later that the game has changed. Even in New Zealand, I think that the penny has dropped, and therefore they are going to be that much more difficult to beat this season because they have players to play 15-man rugby. The only doubt that I have is about their midfield players, but I'll come to that in a moment.

Just for a moment, I would like to revert to the excellence of the rucking in New Zealand. They do it exceedingly well. Their body positions are good. As I have suggested, I think that we haven't stressed enough the body position of going low into a ruck, almost as if the forward concerned was going into a tight scrummage. The best New Zealand forwards drive into the ruck parallel to the side line. This is important, the drive down the line, so that people are not shoving in different directions. They have all learned since their childhood how to build up the drive to create a cutting edge. It is difficult to get our players to do this. They find the short cuts. They arrive and then tend to come in at an angle and it is usually the wrong angle which dissipates the force at their impact. The right angle is to come in parallel to the side line, driving low, and you will find All Blacks when they are between five and seven yards from the ruck instinctively finding the right line and formation and driving over the ball. Every single ruck may be different but All Blacks are marvellous at getting the ball back.

Now this is an attitude of mind. They are determined when they get into that ruck that the ball will come back and lots of little things happen. You see hands all over the place until the ball comes back. If they infringe the law occasionally, well, that's life. They know they are infringing the law and it is up to the referee to stop them. To our referees, may I say this? New Zealand are far better at refereeing the rucks and the mauls than we are in this country. If a player wants to kill a ruck, and it still happens far too often in the British Isles, he will go over the top of the ball and he will sit on it or block it. Well, he won't sit on it long in New Zealand, believe you me. Nobody will. We tried very hard to stand on our feet and ruck, but the Lions still came off the field with their backs looking like a ploughed field, with red weals all over. It happened game after game. Well, fair enough. This is the way New Zealanders play it. If one of their own men has the misfortune to find himself at the bottom of the ruck they will trample on him as well. They believe in this. It is part of their game. And what I'm afraid of is this, that unless our referees referee the rucks well this coming season, some players are going to be in trouble and it may well be the All Blacks, and it may well not be their fault. I hope this does not happen. There will be instances when they will be scraping, looking for this ball and scraping on bodies, and they may well be given an early shower. Don't get me wrong, I'm not saying that all our referees are bad at refereeing the ruck. I notice a great improvement in the last six months. But I'd like to see further improvement and I think our game would be so much better for it. There would be far more continuity and fluidity.

So much for the scrummage, the line-out and the ruck. What is the New Zealander's attitude of mind as far as the tactics of the game are concerned? Usually it is this. In a nutshell, our strength is in our pack, therefore we will play to our pack as often as possible. How do they do this? Their scrum-halves play very close to the set piece. The great thing in New Zealand is to break as near to the set piece as possible. Therefore they have to have flankers who are alert to the possibility of a scrum-half break. They rarely think in terms of their fly-half out there, or they haven't in recent years. In other words, you need a strong tackler like Barry John who can look after his opposite number! Either that, or the No. 8 has to come across to tidy up for the fly-half. Let the back row forwards get on with it. They are sufficiently intelligent to work out a system of defence for themselves, knowing that if you are playing against the All Blacks Sid Going is always likely to break close to the scrum. He will be running forward, and he will want to link in with Kirkpatrick, Wyllie or Sutherland rather than cut to his backs and then the machine starts going.

Now unless you stop the machine before it gets over the gain line, you are likely to be in trouble. From the base of the scrum, from the line-out - from the back of the line-out in particular - and from the ruck, we found, and again it takes a bit of time for these things to penetrate, you must have your last forward coming up to the ruck standing out of it. You cannot afford to have the eighth man in it. He must stand out. But on which side? Well, I used to tell the boys, "On the open side, please." Then it allowed the scrum-half to look after his opposite number. It was nice in that third test when Mervyn went through the back of a lineout, we set up a ruck, we changed the direction of the attack and used the narrow side. Wyllie was the last man to the ruck, we won it and gave the ball to Gareth. Gareth moved to the narrow side and Gerald scored in the corner. That was a classic New Zealand try and what a delight it was to present a classic New Zealand try at Wellington. The only bit wrong with it was that John Pullin was on the wrong side of the ruck, but we'll forgive him for that.

So the pattern in New Zealand was of scrum-halves breaking close and fly-halves kicking. Obviously the fly-halves moved the ball occasionally but the one great ploy was to kick the ball in front of the pack. The wings do not see much of the ball. Now this was a great sadness really, when they had a player of the calibre of Bryan Williams, who I would consider to be world class. The only time you really saw Bryan was in the final Test, when he played well. At first they even played him in the centre! Good! Marvellous!!! He achieved nothing. It was a different story in the fourth Test, when he showed glimpses of the world class player he is. But this is where New Zealand rugby, in my opinion, has gone wrong. They do not believe in the quick transference of ball from scrum-half to wing. It rarely happens and therefore for that reason we rarely found an attacking full-back in that country. The only one that we saw, and Doug Smith has mentioned him already, was Evan Taylor. For my money, and I think the boys agree, Evan was an excellent running, attacking full-back. Well, the possibility of this sort of play isn't there unless you have players, as Mike Gibson and John Dawes have said, that can do it. As a coach my job is to get players doing the basics well. It takes hours, weeks, months, even years to get some players to do these things well. I think the artist in the basic skills of tackling, catching and passing has always been John Dawes. An ability like that in midfield allows other players to express themselves. But we still have players in our first class clubs who cannot perform basic skills. It looks the most simple thing in the world but it isn't. It is a very difficult thing to do for a centre to catch and give, and to get the ball moving rapidly from scrum half to wing.

Remember that try against North Auckland? David Duckham scored it. He ran beautifully and beat two or three men with only inches to spare, only a few inches in which to move and he only had that because John Williams came into the line and beat the man to man-marking by just flicking the ball on with the back of his hands. The ball went like lightening to Dave Duckham. There was never a try on were it not for that quickness, that sleight of hand, that fingertip passing.

Of course in the three-two, four-three, two-one overlap situation you can still have your beautiful fall away pass. I know it is aesthetic. I know it graces and charms all rugby books that we have had for thirty years. It is in the finest public school tradition but, God, it is useless half the time.

I don't think it is my duty as a coach to tell backs like the Lions had what moves they should use; the miss moves and the scissors and this, that and the other. Let them create for themselves! Damn it all, little kids of 7 and 8 years of age back home in Wales will jink and dummy and all the rest of it. That's bonus! But can he move the ball on in one movement?

I'll never forget the Wednesday before the final Test in New Zealand. I had been working with the pack on one field for about an hour and on the other field the prima donnas were practising. Nobody had watched the forwards but hundreds of people were watching the backs. I said to the forwards, "Excuse me now? Carry on. I want to see what they are doing over there. They are probably playing soccer but I might as well go over there and see what is happening."

To my delight Sydney was doing some rugby ploys - I think he had only just started, mind! I said, "What is happening?" "Oh," he said, "we are doing the North Auckland dummy scissors move."

"Good, let us have a look at it," I said. The three Going brothers were playing for North Auckland and Sid gave the ball to his brother, Brian I think, at fly-half who gave it, I think to the inside centre, who did a scissors with Ken, at full-back, who came back towards the strength, towards the pack and Sid had slowed down his progress - I was waiting for this. Then he did another scissors with Ken and only a magnificent tackle by John Williams prevented a score. It probably saved the game for us.

John Dawes has always been the master of the timing and the execution of a pass. A model for youngsters to copy…

"Let us have a look at it, John," I said. And they did it. "Let's build on it," I said.

"Three scissors, four scissors, five scissors."

Imagine the crowd by this time. Horror on their faces! We were meeting their little darlings on the Saturday, for the final Test, and here we were demonstrating, showing off like mad, finishing off with seven scissors on the trot. Drunk with power!

All I am saying is that you can do anything in the world provided you have the players who can take the ball and pass it, who can handle. Then ploys are easy; the moves, the gimmicks, call them what you like. It does not need a creative genius to work out a few moves. Let them be a part of the players themselves. If you've got mid-field players, who are you as coach to tell them what moves they should try? Let them create for themselves. Then by all means have a good look at it and say, "Yes, that's not bad, perhaps this way is better, do you think?" They won't think but at least you can ask them to and at least they are creating for themselves and in a match situation, under pressure, they will use the moves because, after all, they have thought of them. It is the duty of the coach to look after the basics.

It is in this area that I think New Zealand might come unstuck. Mike Gibson never said it, because he is too modest a chap - but privately and quietly to me he has said on more than one occasion, "When they move this ball in mid-field, I can usually take two players and sometimes three, because the passing is so bad."

The ball was delivered too high, or too low, or back on the hip so that there wasn't any slickness. It was ponderous. The All Blacks' backs moved their feet quickly enough but the execution of the pass was not good enough and very often the play wasn't ticking over quickly enough either, so it was easy to counter, or it was with the mid-field players that New Zealand put out against us.

But to counter the way the Lions moved the ball along the line was a very difficult thing, because the execution was so good. Please forgive me for stressing this, but it is essentially a very simple game. It is a question of resolving the complexities and the simplicities. This is the whole purpose of teaching. The bad teacher will make everything sound terribly complicated; you don't know where the hell you are by the time he's finished with it. Well, that is the province of the coach too. He must resolve all that is difficult into something simple. It is basically a simple game and when you get people doing the simplicities, well, then you can add your seven scissors and you are back to your complexities. The whole purpose of asking the boys to compile statistics was to get them looking at a game in a certain way. Now we can all go and watch a game and we can all look at it differently, and we may well have seen a different game. Ex-referees often go and see it and when you talk to them after the match they will talk to you about refereeing. Ray McLoughlin I am sure when he goes will observe the intricacies of front row play, and that confrontation he finds terrifically exciting. He may not be amused by the delicate side-step of the mid-field player. Since, for every match 19 were involved, fifteen players and four subs., there were eleven not doing anything really but just watching the game and unless it's a trained mind, they'd watch it overall and get an impression. I think that this is a tendency of a lot of people who watch this game in this manner. As spectators we watch and after the game somebody comes up to you and they say, "The tight prop on the Red side played a good game, didn't he?" And we look frightfully intelligent and we say, "Yes, he did, didn't he?" thinking like mad - we don't really remember what kind of a game the prop had.

Therefore I now ask the boys to compile statistics related to their own particular game. In other words, one was asking their eyes to look at a particular sphere of the game right the way through which would be of help to them in the next match or the match after that, and they looked at it, I would say, through the eyes of an authority. I could then go to the person who was compiling the line-out count. What ball did he win? Who was throwing it in that time? What resulted from that particular line-out, and you know you had quite a lot of statistics which were quite valuable. But the important thing was that that man had looked very closely at an area in which he was frightfully interested. I find with a squad of 26, or whatever it is, I like watching a game in their company, particularly when there are young players just coming into the team and you can talk them into the game, or you can let them talk you into the game - let them themselves talk you into the game. In other words they tell you if the person in his position did the right thing or the wrong thing. That, I think, is a useful way of watching a match.

Now I want to deal with the question of counter attack. Let us say that we have a set-piece and it is the All Blacks' ball. From that set-piece the All Blacks' fly-half will often put the ball back into the box. Your own men will be lying pretty flat, but with the full-back and the blind side wing properly positioned, you are well placed to take advantage of a ball which the opposition has given to you. The Lions won less than 40 per cent of the ball most of the time, so if the opposition are dull enough to kick the ball to you then you must take advantage of it. You have a full-back and you have a wing. The full-back should position himself so that he can run in to the ball to give himself momentum and he must also choose the right angle. When John Williams took a ball in that situation, he had to have the help of his blind side wing. This is the whole basis of setting up the counter attack. But beyond that, the full-back must be prepared to take advantage of his support. It wasn't easy with John Williams because John has a lot of the New Zealander in him. John loves having a go at the opposition, but it mustn't be. If the full-back does that, then the chances are he will spoil a good ball.

The second thing is that when the full-back catches the ball, he then gives it to the wing coming inside but the wing himself must time his supporting run and give a pass properly. This is very important and I have found myself shouting often, "Switch the target! Switch the target!" meaning, of course, that eight pairs of eyes are glued on the full-back, and they are running towards him and they are looking forward to the confrontation, but he takes and he gives and he changes the target. Then you want the wing also to give the ball. Thus you change the target again.

It is very difficult, you know, for the Mullers of this world to think in terms of two targets. When it comes to three or four or five targets, well good God! This is in the realm of nuclear physics. So you change your target as often as you can. The difficulty invariably comes from the threequarters who have been lying up flattish in defence. They have to be linked in and to do that, they have to MOVE. The Lions' backs loved playing soccer, and why shouldn't they? It is a good game, it teaches balance, it teaches lots of things. The most important thing it teaches is running off the ball. We had heard statistics of even a player like Barry John only having the ball for a little over a minute in the whole match. What does he do for the rest of the time? He should be working off the ball. It is so important, therefore, that threequarters who have been deployed in defence should retire to a position where they can counter-attack. So even the blind-side wing must link with the other backs at the right angle of run. The more I have to do with this game the more I appreciate that it is a game of angles. Often you find a wing threequarter running at the wrong angle. I had one on tour. I worked for hours trying to get him to run at the right angle because he wasn't giving himself a chance. He wasn't giving himself the option of either going outside or inside. It is the angle that matters. It must not be too wide and yet he doesn't want to run straight down the field, or he is going to run back into an area congested with forwards. If he does that, I think that the best thing is for the wing to link with the inside centre, or second five-eighth. But not the fly-half. It is very difficult for the fly-half to do this if you work out the angle. Now, don't for one minute accept that as being definitive, work it out for yourselves.

It depends on the players that you have, how they think, how they react. But the important thing is that the backs who had been lying up have to work pretty hard to get back into position. Once they do that the counter-attack is on. But tell your fly-half, "Look, I don't expect you to take the ball from the wing but I expect you to slip across so that you can come in further out." So, running off the ball is a very important manoeuvre.

I would also like to say that I found it particularly useful, when I was working with the forwards, to get them to retire themselves and to set up situations so that the backs could counter-attack. Throw the ball behind the forwards in practice, make them run back, then the first forward has to fall on the ball and get up.

It is a skill that we practised for hours, for the simple reason that you cannot lie on the ball in New Zealand. Falling on the ball does not mean a holiday. You have to go down and get up straight away. This is hard work. If you are carrying 16 or 17 stone you try it out with your players. Down, Up - Down, Up - Down, Up - Down, Up. It's not easy. The first man has to run back 20 yards, go down, get up with the ball, slip it to the next guy, and so on. This gives you continuity. Eventually, one of them decides, "Right, we'll have a maul," and then out comes the ball and your backs are away. By doing this, I am convinced that our cover defence improved no end and probably saw us through the first Test, because we had done so much of this kind of work. We were so used to running backwards into rucks, that in the first test, when we seemed to be running back a hell of a lot, we were able to run back and still keep poised to tackle like hell. It took a lot of guts but the fact that we had done it so much in training carried us through. It is also worth remembering that if you can ruck after going back twenty or thirty yards, then it is reasonable to assume that you are a good rucking pack going forward. You should not practise rucks with your pack going forward all the time. It is far better exercise to ruck making them go backwards, and the other thing very often is that while the forwards are working so hard, the backs are enjoying themselves but you can often catch them out because they have not been running off the ball. That must be put to them at all times in training. They must be caught out and seen not to get back into position to maintain the counter attack. This, then, is the province of the counter-attack as far as the forwards are concerned. The build-up of the counter-attack is from two situations - one from the full-back and the other from the forwards.

From this, it is obvious that the winger now has much more of a footballer's game to play. He is no longer just a runner-in of tries, but the difficulty is that he has always been a different animal now, a different breed! In so many situations now, he is the pivot of your attack and he becomes effectively your fly-half. Well, I know that this is a problem. However, wings these days must have the qualities of a full-back, in tidying up and running the ball out of defence. They must be able to take the ball, turn towards the touch line, and hand it to another player in support. Either that, or he must take the ball from the full back, and then he becomes the pivot of your attack. He's your fly-half. Therefore he must be a person who can pass the ball. As we are still in a transitional stage as far as wingers are concerned, this is a great deal to ask. Therefore, I would agree with John Dawes 100 per cent in what he said. Although you want an attacker as a full-back, he must be first and foremost a full-back. He must be able to vary his entry into the line, sometimes between the two centres, sometimes between the outside centre and the wing, sometimes purely running behind the wing for an inside pass or an outside pass, but he must be there running five yards or so behind his wing. These things vary, according to the full-back that you have, but he must still be a full-back. He must be able to think for himself, and he must work hard in training so that he and his wingers can get to know one another's play and have confidence in one another. If they are prepared to run and work hard off the ball then, obviously, they will be a success.

We have always thought of wings as being runners-in, fleet-footed players who can score the tries but these days we expect far more from them. We expect some of the qualities of full-backs, we expect them in certain situations even to be distributors like a fly-half. The game is changing virtually every day. I am sure that we have not explored all the full-back possibilities open to us. There is scope for the creative mind. I am pleased at the way the game is developing because it allows players to play in more than one position. I would strongly advise schoolmaster coaches not to tell a boy when he is eleven or twelve that he is a fly-half. He is nothing of the kind! Play him at full-back, play him at centre so that he learns the intricacies of the hospital pass, and then he will learn when to give the ball, he will then learn something about timing.

If you play him at full-back, he will get to know something about the blind spots that a full-back has, and believe you me there are plenty, then when he goes back to full-back he will be able to put that ball on a sixpence and find the blind spots of a full-back if he is an attacking kicker of any kind at all. Play him on the wing too, particularly if he has a selfish streak in him. Then he will realise that wings do like seeing the ball. Martin Turner nods his head and agrees with me, but there were days, Martin, when wings hardly saw the ball at all. I think that in 43 international matches that Ken Jones played for Wales he saw the ball about 44 times. These days wings are constantly in the game and they have to work. They have to work off the ball. There are so many avenues that they can explore.

Now then, the final question is: "Are we happy with this kind of pattern of play?" I think it does have expression to the people we are. I think it does justice to the personality of this nation, and I use 'nation' now in the full concept of four nations. It does give expression to the British character.

I remember going around clubs about ten years ago and saying: I will talk about the New Zealand pattern, I will talk as well as I can about the South African pattern and I am sorry I cannot talk about the British pattern because there isn't any. Perhaps there isn't any now, I don't know. John Taylor has implied that there is. I think there is. And I think it does give expression to the way we want to play our game.

The All Blacks will come in October. We must be alert, as Doug rightly said. We want to give them a warm welcome, they deserve it. The New Zealander believes in himself. That was the finest quality that I saw in these people. "You've won the first game," they said, "so what! Wait until you go to Wanganui." We beat them at Wanganui by twenty-odd points, "Wait till you get to Waikato." So it went on throughout the tour, and by the end they said, "Mm! Yes, you may have won the series but you wait until you come back next time - 1977." This spirit - that they cannot lose – is the spirit that they believe in themselves. I think it is time that we believed in ourselves. England have just done an excellent job in South Africa, an excellent job. I don't think we always appreciate that the standards in this country have improved enormously during the past three or four years. It is up to us to make sure that we maintain these standards and better them even further. I think we all have a part to play, and possibly the most important aspect of rugby football is the psychological side of it. Once that is right, once the approach and the attitude is right then I know that we have the technical skill to put it across, and we've got the players. It is up to us.

Bob Hiller has talked about the pressure on players. There are lots of pressures. It is up to us coaches to take away as many of those pressures as possible. I think, the more one sees of this game, the more one appreciates that the psychological side is probably the most important side of coaching. At any rate that is my impression judging from my observations on tour and with a first-class club. It probably applies at school level too.

Q. There are three points to this question. We have been told that the game has changed and the New Zealanders learnt a lot from us. Yet the series, after all, was 2 - 1 - 1 and depended in the end on goal-kicking.

(1) Do you honestly feel that the same tactics would have been successful, assuming we were playing under today's laws, against the '63 or '67 All Blacks. In other words, was it a poor All Blacks side we played against?

(2) What change in tactics would you, or could you have made if in fact we had lost the first two Tests?

and

(3) Why was Ray McLoughlin sent home after breaking his thumb, when he was such an asset as a coach and would have been fit for the final test?

A. The last question first. We had an edict from the Four Home Unions' committee that if somebody was injured and could take no further part in the tour then whoever he may have been, he should go home. That was some thing in the tour agreement, and we had to abide by it. We would have loved to have had Ray with us for all the time because his contribution was enormous.

Now, you asked if we had lost the first two Tests, would we have changed our tactics. We certainly changed them quite a bit after the second Test and we lost that one. I think that in losing the second we discovered that we had the winning of the third and fourth. My disappointment on tour was that we did not win the fourth. I felt that we should have done. We were 8 points down in no time at all, we came back, we had the wind behind us and sun in our backs, and we gained the psychological advantage of coming back from 8 nil, right on half-time to 8 all. After two or three minutes in the second half Muller did some-thing stupid yet again and gave us a penalty. We were 11 - 8 up and that was the moment I felt when we could have relaxed and played our natural game. But we didn't and this was a bitter disappointment to me. I think that there was so much at stake and the boys felt this right through the game.

Anyway, this kind of question "if" is always a very difficult one. Obviously you look at every game as it comes. We vowed that we would take every game as it came, every game, just the next one mattered. What happened before that was history, we were not interested. I will never forget Willie John - we were at Queenstown at about five o'clock and we were watching the telerecording of the first test the previous day. We were all gathered around the television set, and suddenly a face appeared at the door with a drink in his hand and said, "Gentlemen, it is all history, forget about it." That was Willie John. And probably so true. In other words you took the next game as it came along and the next one. Certainly after the second test we changed our tactics quite a bit, and I think we have mentioned areas in which we did change our tactics.

And your third question. It is awfully difficult to compare teams from different areas. I never like doing this. You men tion '63 and '67. They were very good New Zealand teams - I have yet to see a poor New Zealand team and you will not see a poor New Zealand side next year. Whether in 1971 they were up to the calibre of the 1967 is another matter. Personally I don't think they were - that was a world class side, the '67 one - but they were not unbeatable. They should have lost to the Barbarians. They should have lost to East Wales. Some of our teams did have the beating of that side and I would say that some of our teams will have the beating on the next New Zealand side too. That is the only frame of mind in which we can go into these games.

Q. *Obviously the relationship between yourself and the captain on the Lions' tour must have been ideal. When I started coaching it was a dirty word. You were one jump above the groundsman. However, the status of coaches in clubs has still to be established, and I feel that this conference could do a tremendous amount by making useful suggestions in relation to this captain/coach relationship, particularly as to what extent thecoach will be involved in selection, and included on committees because, after all, he is the technology man in the Club.*

A. This is a very interesting question. I believe that rugby football is a dictatorship. I think there is only one man in the club who can have the vision. Coaching means having a vision, seeing a pattern. Only one man can do that. I played in an era when there were thirteen men picking the Llanelli side. The question that one of them always asked was, "Why is the full-back standing so far back?" You see you cannot have people contributing to that extent! I work on the principle that if I want selectors to work with me, I will invite one or two advisers who are kindred spirits. Obviously there are certain people in the club you could not possibly work with. There are some selectors who do not know a great deal about rugby football, but it is amazing how many people want to be selectors. This is the glamour job of rugby football. In every club - even at international level - the ambition, the burning ambition is created by the power people think they have if they are made selectors, and these days, with the advent of the squad system it does not mean a thing. You don't NEED selectors. I would say I have got about 26 first team squad players at Llanelli and I pick the team with the captain and usually about two others just before we go out to training at about 7 o'clock. If the four have arrived by five to seven it will take us two minutes flat to pick the team for the next game. But I know that there are still some clubs who will sit down for two hours on a Monday night to pick a team. You may have difficulty if there are three or four sides in the club. Then you have to look at it a bit more closely, but the actual selection these days does not mean a thing. Even at national level, I would say, you could probably pick the Welsh team in five minutes - you've got your squad. Once that has been picked leading up to an international, you know who your 15 are. It doesn't need selection.

The coach must find his place in the club. He is an important man, and for that reason he should be given 100% support by all the committee men and all the workers there. He should work in close conjunction with his captain, obviously, because after all he must NOT interfere when the team is on the field. The captain is there to carry out what has been discussed previously. Obviously he will change tactics if it is necessary so there must be complete confidence, the one in the other.

In New Zealand, the coach is a very important man in the set-up. As yet he is not terribly important in the British Isles

- not sufficiently important. In about a fortnight, I am to run a coaching course somewhere in England for a county. We will be doing this course on a first-class club's ground, and yet that first-class club has not got a coach. I don't know the hell why I am going to that county to coach, when the top-class club doesn't even have a coach itself. I don't see the sense of it and I must admit I am surprised that there are so many leading English clubs that still do not have a coach. Well, it is in your hands! Carry the gospel! The Welsh are so smug, I know…

Q. *You say that if you kick the ball, you give the other side possession to counter-attack. I have always thought that the strength of the French game is that they use the cross-kick very effectively and it is a tactic which is not used very much in England. Perhaps you feel it is an unwise move.*

A. No, I'd be all for it. I'm a great believer in the tactical kick. I regret very much that the grubber isn't used as nicely these days as it was a few years ago. It is done beautifully by some people, but these days one hardly sees the grub kick. I coach it myself because I think it is an excellent way of penetrating a line close on you.

I think that the cross-kick is not easy but if it is done well I think it is an excellent ploy. However, it is essential to get players to spend hours practising it. The other thing, of course, is - and this probably is the most important thing - that we are such animals that if we do something well once or twice, perhaps there is a tendency for us to do it a bit too often. That is the difficulty you are going to have with your wing. If your wing develops into a great cross-kicker, then possibly for the rest of his days this will be satisfaction for him and he may lose the desire to run for the corner, or to give the inside pass, or to look for the full-back in support. Kicking is a good slave but a very bad master.

I went through one season at school almost having given up hope for rugby football. I think it was a protest against rugby football in general, particularly at first class level - I'm taking you back now about 8 or 10 years. There was so much kicking in our game, people were going through the centre and kicking it away. There was this psychological barrier, and for that season I told the boys at my school: "Nobody; NOBODY is going to kick for the rest of the season, the whole season. They ran and ran and ran, and in the end they enjoyed it. They didn't think about kicking and they didn't want to kick. You had to break down this psychological barrier but, having said that, I would appreciate that, used well, obviously it is a good thing to have and one can enjoy good kicking enormously.

Barry John made some beautiful kicks on tour. I would say that he was the best player I have seen for cutting the line. I don't think we practise this sufficiently. Outside the 25, getting that bounce and into touch. George Nepia - I had a great deal of his company - I read somewhere that George would go out, he'd put a handkerchief about a yard from the touchline and then he'd kick from twenty, thirty, forty, fifty yards and get that ball to land on the handkerchief.

Q. *How did you set up the mauls?*

A. The basic was to get the ball carrier running in the proper body position. New Zealand can show us all the way in this respect. You can easily pick out an All Black. You could probably even do it in the street. If you see any large, hard gentleman, of ominous visage, walking down a street as if he was leaning into a gale, with one shoulder thrust forward, the chances are that he is an All Black! They do this when they drive into mauls. They lean forward, with one shoulder thrust ahead and with the ball carried on the trailing hip so that it is as far away as possible from the shoulder which takes the impact of the body contact.

Our forwards are not nearly so conscious of the correct body position in rucks and mauls. A lot of them are terribly upright in the way they run. Certainly I have two or three forwards in the Llanelli team who run so upright I am not sure whether they look more like male models or children!

I think this stems from the period in this country that Ray McLoughlin referred to, when we were much too conscious of turning when we reached the point of body contact, so that we could give the ball to a supporting player. Ray mentioned a certain gentleman on the Lions' tour of 1966. Turning is not a bad thing, as long as a decisive, driving shoulder charge has been made first. If that first charge is not checked, then the forward should drive on until it is. This achieves maximum committal. That is the moment to turn and to make the ball available for the next man.

Once the physical contact and the committal have been achieved, the next man up should bind on to the ball carrier to start to form a wedge and to give the support necessary for the man to stay on his feet. As John Taylor said, that support should be instantaneous. With All Black packs, it almost invariably is. That then creates a platform for the other forwards to build on, filling in on each side of the ball as they arrive so that the forward who distributes the ball to the scrum-half achieves maximum control.

I got the forwards to simulate match conditions in practiceby starting the pack in one corner, with eight opposition forwards strung out at intervals diagonally across the length and breadth of the field. When the pack arrived at the first man, they would drive into him and turn and get the ball back. While they were doing that, the first opposition forward doubled back to the next man so that by the time the pack arrived at the second situation, they had two forwards to drive into instead of one.

This process was repeated all the way down and across the field so that the pack that was mauling or rucking the ball found that the opposition was getting firmer and firmer all the way as the opposition forwards doubled back to add themselves to each succeeding barrier, until at the end there were eight opposition forwards waiting to take the impact of the pack that was working with the ball.

The problem of coaching schoolboys is different. They don't have hands big enough to control the ball so easily with one hand and because of the severe physical contact which is involved in the exercise, I don't think it is fair to ask small boys to really put their shoulder in. It is better for them to turn until they acquire the physical capacity to drive, but the essence of creating the platform and binding is still the same.

I would like to reiterate that despite what was said while we were in New Zealand, particularly just after the Canterbury game, the Lions did NOT try to lie on the ball to kill it. From the very beginning of our preparation at Eastbourne, we tried as hard as we could to keep on our feet and to make the ball available. We never matched the All Blacks in the rucks, and there were times when we were beaten in that phase of the game by a provincial team - most notably by Otago - but I think we did very much better than British touring teams have in the past. However, it is an area of the game where we in Britain still have to do a lot of very hard work.

Q. *How did you feel when you were appointed assistant manager and coach of the British Lions?*

A. The first thing was a feeling of humility. I had not been good enough as a player to represent the Lions myself, and to find myself in this position coaching the side was something that I looked forward to enormously.

I spent a number of weekends with Doug Smith at his home in Essex. We were able to discuss previous Lions' tours, and to discuss the All Blacks in some depth. Then we sounded the views of as many people as possible. I also watched as much film of the All Blacks as I could, so that I was able to come to certain conclusions about the All Blacks pattern of play. As a coach, you have to analyse the opposition and I also read a great deal, although I was a bit disappointed in the number of books that had been turned out in New Zealand. I wished there had been more. One of the most interesting was Dave Gallaher's book, which was published back in 1905. Amazingly, a lot of what is written in that book is relevant at the present time. It shows, I think, that the All Blacks tend to be more conservative than we are in this country. They found a successful pattern of play and they have clung on to it.

I got as many journals as possible from New Zealand, and what I found particularly useful when it came down to preparing the actual detail for our tour was to read very meticulously the New Zealand Almanacks for the last three or four years, because this did allow me to seethe strength of the different provinces in New Zealand. Obviously, some variation occurs but it was interesting to me to work out how many All Blacks, how many trialists and so on played for the different provinces. This enabled me to rough out my teams very much in advance. We also picked the brains of everyone who knew something about the New Zealand pattern of play. We invited John Dawes, long before he was thought of as captain. We talked to Don Rutherford and Ray Williams and we had papers from the other people. It was a very worthwhile exercise. Whatever my views were, they needed confirmation. Any ideas that I had about New Zealand scrummaging, about New Zealand line-out play, about any details, all needed this confirmation from other people who thought in depth about the game.

Q. *You obviously think that it is essential for the manager, the coach and the captain to get on well together?*

A. Yes, it is, very much so. It is so important that there aren't clashes of personality and that people can work together. Doug Smith and myself were really fortunate with our players. It is nice to put on record that I never heard a cross word between any two players in the three and a half months that we were out in New Zealand, which is quite incredible really.

Q. *The Four Home Unions, up to now, have not allowed the coach of the Lions team to sit in on selection. Do you agree with this?*

A. No. I feel very strongly that when a coach is on tour, and he is in charge of the playing side, obviously his feelings about different players matter a great deal. He is also in a position to exercise a great deal of influence as far as selection is actually concerned for the tour games. Therefore, I feel that, for future tours, it is important that the Assistant Manager should take part in the initial selection, because to be in charge of the playing side, he will have a pattern of play in his own mind.

Do you pick your players to fit in with a pattern, or do you allow other people to pick players for you and then start from scratch to find a pattern? I make no apology for saying this, but I feel that rugby football has to be a dictatorship. The man who puts those players on the field has got in his own mind's eye the pattern of play he wants. He is responsible for the pattern, therefore to a large extent, he should be responsible for selecting the players for that pattern. The role of the other selectors, I am afraid, ought to be subservient to the coach himself. I must say that before we left these shores, John Tallent, as chairman of the Four Home Unions' Tours Committee, brought us together and he told us what our functions were going to be. This was good. We knew exactly what we were about. I was told, obviously, that it was my job to be assistant to Doug, and that if anythinghappened to Doug then, automatically I would be manager, but Doug was to be the boss at all times. Now the playing side of it was completely in my hands and therefore, I had to work very closely with the captain. There can never be any success unless the captain and the coach work well together. This applies very much on tour, and it applies to club and county rugby as well.

I must also say that in the months preceding the tour, I was always invited to the meetings of the selectors, and I was invited to express an opinion, but when it eventually came to the business of selecting the Lions' side, I wasn't there at all - it was the four National selectors, with Doug in the chair. I think this should be changed.

New Zealand accepted this many years ago. Their coach is the chairman of the selectors. He has with him virtually what are a couple of advisors. I agree with that, because the fewer people that you have on selection, the better are your chances of having a successful side. After all, you are only going to get a successful side if your coach has done his homework and can pick the right players to fit in and play to the right pattern.

Q. *If you have a three man selection committee, how can you really know if you've got the best players in your side?*

A. In Wales, it is easy. I really do not understand why they still persist with trials. These are quite unnecessary. They have a squad system going, and they add on or take away from the squad, holding say, a couple of squad sessions in the months preceding the international match. That is quite sufficient. It is not necessary to have a trial system at all.

However, I confess that with England it is a bit more difficult, because of the geography of the country. Then your chairman of selectors and possibly your coach ask people in different areas whom they know on the same wave-length as they are to assist them. These people will know exactly the type of pattern the coach wants to play, and the type of player who is wanted.

From this, you could build up your squad in the first couple of months of your season and, say, a month or so before the actual international match, you could start your practices without reference to the normal English trial system. I don't think this is necessary at all. It is completely out of date as far as I can see. It only cuts across the county and the club system.From the squad, it is easy to carry on and find the right side of your International fifteen. I know there are difficulties of working these things out, but I think this is the kind of pattern that is necessary. In Wales at the present moment, selection is quite easy. Whether it is by accident or design or by very clever working out - I don't know, but they have a squad, and all they have to do is add one or two players per season. The team then more or less picks itself.

Q. *You would not subscribe to the view that says: "We've got six selectors, we pick what we think are the best players and we then hand them over to the coach and we then say, 'There you are coach, make the best of them!'"*

A. That is mediaeval thinking!

Q. *What pattern of rugby did you really aim for with the Lions, because obviously, you had formulated a fairly clear idea in your own mind of what New Zealand would do?*

A. First of all, look at the New Zealand pattern. I thought it was fairly predictable. It hasn't changed much in the last ten years. One might argue, "Well, why should it?" because for so many years it has produced winning rugby. I think that we were very lucky in 1971 that this kind of archaic thinking was still persisting in New Zealand. Fortunately, as far as we were concerned, there had been certain changes in law, and these changes in law, not appreciated then by New Zealand, had demanded a different approach to the game.

There is no doubt that the ruck has been the creative contribution of New Zealand to world rugby. Their whole game is geared to the ruck situation. In 1967 for instance, in Freddie Allen's side, they worked out patterns from the set play of line-out and set scrummage, in order to set up the ruck situation. For instance, they wheeled the set scrummage slightly so that when they worked the ball out and MacRae took a tackle, their pack would be that much nearer to support. Having rucked the ball, they would work back to the narrow side of the field. So even their set piece play was geared to the ruck situation.

New Zealand then went out to South Africa. Claassens was the South African coach. He worked this out in detail. In fact he thought probably along two different lines, but the line that received the greater publicity was the one in which he picked "Joggie" Jansen to out-MacRae MacRae. Well, New Zealand, like any other side, are great at going forward and not so marvellous at going backwards. So that was one of Claassens' answers. I felt that you could take the imitative by superior scrummaging, and this is where we worked really hard. You must use as much brain power as you have around you, and I was very fortunate in that respect. We allowed our players, and particularly people with experience, people like Ray McLoughlin, to have a great deal of say in this respect. As far as the scrummaging side of the work was concerned, people like McLoughlin and so on were there to help other players. We went through it meticulously and found that by about the first or second week in New Zealand, we could produce a

173

shove that would have upset any plans at all about wheeling the scrummage. I think the evidence is there on film. You even found in the test matches that the Lions were able, occasionally, by exerting an eight man shove, to move the New Zealand pack backwards fairly quickly. In the second Test, we found that even though we had shoved them back about eight yards, Sid Going was still able to breach our back row defence, the point being that our back row had stayed down. From that moment on, we found that once the shove had been started and the scrum was really rolling, the momentum could be sustained by six forwards, so the two flankers disengaged themselves from the scrummage.

The point I am making is that we were very much aware of the possible wheel by the All Blacks. This would have been to our great disadvantage but they couldn't do it as long as our scrummage was tight. It was something that we worked terribly hard on in training. We would often scrummage for 40 minutes. Once we did more than an hour. But it was never static. We worked up and down the field with running as well as scrummaging.

Q. *Forty minutes of scrummaging would shatter an awful lot of first-class players. Did you use a scrummaging machine out there? Did you use local opposition? Or did you just stick to the actual members of the party?*

A. I stuck to the members of the party. They knew that this was a severe part of the training. This is why I emphasise the fact that we did scrummaging practice two days before the match. We never did it on the day before a match. We knew, though, that we could achieve an actual and a psychological advantage through scrum-maging, because it is a physical thing, me versus you, and everybody else on the field can see who is winning. For that reason, the boys were quite prepared to work hard at it. I know that there were some occasions when they were virtually on their knees. But I still carried on and even after that I would do about ten minutes or a quarter of an hour of ruck practice. The only difficulty about ruck practice, of course, is that you have to be very careful that you don't have injuries. You can't afford to have injuries on a training ground.

With a game two days away, one could afford to be more severe. This scrummage practice usually came, in any case, after the week-end and on a Saturday the boys did let their hair down a bit, so it was important to have a hard training session. I can see them quite vividly now - the sweat pouring off them during this scrum exercise. Up in Waitangi, they really suffered!

You see, even after a Wednesday game they would have a few drinks, but still usually there was cause for some small celebration and so the reimposition of discipline was an important part of our training. And in reimposing that discipline, we were achieving something which helped us to break the All Blacks' pattern of play. Our scrummaging helped us to nullify another of the strengths of New Zealand rugby, which is their half-back play, or scrum-half play, as we call it here.

I would say that of the sixteen or seventeen scrum-halves who played against us, fourteen or fifteen were good enough to play for their country: Because of the forward power in New Zealand, they breed excellent scrum—halves. But they are scrum-halves who try to cross the gain line. In other words the basic principle in New Zealand is: "Cross the gain line as near to the set piece as possible." From the scrum, from the line-out, from the ruck, the scrum-half must cross the gain line.

Sid Going, of course, was an excellent example. If he could get over that gain line, his back row were in business. When Going was playing well, Kirkpatrick was playing well.

I must thank the Rugby Football Union for having their Centenary when they did, and for bringing all those players over! I went over to Bristol and to Twickenham, and so on, and watched Colin Meads and Sid Going and Ian Kirkpatrick playing. I felt that if we could stop Sid Going, we would also be stopping Kirkpatrick, who is, of course, a world-class player. Therefore, we decided that the last forward up should not go into the ruck. He would stand out on the open side. Our scrum-half, there-fore, would take the narrow side. Usually Sid Going went to the narrow side. This worked well, but Sid was still a difficult man to stop - low centre of gravity; a tough little guy: and, a great scrum-half. One of the two best scrum-halves in the world now that Dawie de Villiers has given up.

So we had to cope with a running scrum-half and usually a kicking standoff. You found this not only at All Black and provincial level, but you found it in schoolboys as well. Too often, far too often, they'd kick away good possession. I seem to recall, even in the Second Test, Sid Going beat a couple of men and he kicked it high to John Williams, who started a counter-attack, out to Mike Gibson, out to Gerald Davies and we scored from our own twenty-five.

With the second five-eighth or inside centre possibly taking the tackle, New Zealand teams tended to have three inside players trying to use the ball. The result, of course, has been that they've lost sight of the value of quick transference of ball from scrum-half to wing. They could not do this - none of them could do it. When we got back, it was interesting to watch some of the films of the tour and how bad the New Zealand handling of the ball was.

Mike Gibson is a humble fellow, but he said, "I can take two of them most times, and sometimes three." They did not have this finger-tip passing which we lay a good deal of stress on, and rarely did we find an attacking full-back. So there wasn't this other dimension which we strived for.

We deliberately tried to play Fergus McCormick out of it, you know. Barry John watched the Canterbury game with me and I said, "Look at Fergie McCormick very closely. Watch his every move." And I seem to recall asking Barry on a Friday - we were playing a game of snooker - and I turned to him and said: "Now don't forget tomorrow." There was no time to talk to Barry in the dressing room. The boys do not want to be bothered then. I said, "Look, do me one favour, I don't want to seethis man playing against us in any more tests," and Barry just did it for me. He played him out of the game.

Then they brought in Laurie Mains, but he was not a great attacker. The best attacking full-back they had was this chap Evan Taylor, who played for the New Zealand Universities against us. However, they did not pick him and they didn't have this other dimension that we had in our game. Our pattern therefore was quite different.

The recent changes in the laws of the game have had a profound effect on the way it is played. You don't have to play the ball with the foot after a tackle, and that has taken away a number of the ruck situations. A player can now pick up the ball and start the process of developing this continuity that one looks for in rugby football. And what is the point nowadays of setting up a ruck from a line-out, when your two lines of backs are twenty yards away from one another? Thirdly, of course, the change of law which has transformed the whole approach to rugby football is the new restriction on touch-kicking. This has created a new dimension in rugby football. It helped the Lions to create a pattern in which we could counter-attack; use a ball that they had given to us. Therefore when all these newspaper men worked out how much possession we had won from set scrums, or line-outs or what have you, I would say, "Please add on another 10% because we are going to have this as a bonus anyway from ball which our opponents in New Zealand will kick away."

Q. *We now know what to expect from New Zealand rugby. How do we beat them in this country?*

A. I think we must lay a great deal of stress on the basics of the game, and particularly the unit skills. There is no question about it, these people can be out-scrummaged, and as I have already inferred, this can spoil a number of things that they try to set up. It will be interesting, of course, to see how they get on with our interpretation of law, and I hope our referees do referee the games to the law. More often than not, we fall over backwards in this country to accommodate touring sides. I think this should be stopped, and referees must be given to understand this. Touring sides come here and they must play to our interpretation. We have to do this in their country, and it is only right that they should do it here, because - make no bones about it - the interpretation is different.

As far as the rucks are concerned, they are a long way ahead of us. We have tried desperately hard, but it will take our boys a few more years before they have the skill and confidence of a New Zealand pack in the loose. After all, this is their creative contribution to the game, and they do it much better than we do.

Where we can beat them, I think, unless they have found a lot of new players, is in this quick transference of ball from scrum-half to wing. We mentioned selection earlier. I've reached the point now where the first thing I look for in a mid-field player, is a person who can take and give a ball quickly in one movement. At one time I used to put the jinkers and the side-steppers, on a pedestal, and then I realised of course that this was whatwas wrong with our rugby. Too often we had not done our homework up front and we'd rely on our Cliff Jones's and our Cliff Morgans to get us out of all sort of difficulties and to win our matches for us. Well, I am very pleased to say that this is a thing of the past. These days you must have people in the middle of the field who can take and give. I think the classic example is John Dawes, and may John carry on playing for another year or two just to show the other players how important this aspect of the game is. He is a classic example and he is the type of player that youngsters can model themselves on. He is not a flashy player by any means, but I am so glad to be able to say that the selectors of the Lions felt, even from the very start of their work, that John Dawes, merely by his play in mid-field, justified selection as a Lion, not just as a Wednesday player, but as a Test player.

Q. *You subscribe therefore to the old adage that the game begins on the wing?*

A. Yes, I do. If you can stretch defences, if you can work the ball swiftly from scrum-half to wing, then you are in business. In this country, our flair is for running, and yet I have thought for a number of years that we have not really had a British pattern. Everyone else had one. The Springboks. The All Blacks. The French. But not us.

That no longer applies. We have found a style of play now. We try to play our rugby up front as hard as they do in New Zealand and South Africa, with a great deal of emphasis on the unit skills and we do those as compe-tently and as scientifically as possible so that we can release our genius which is in running game behind the scrummage. The development of that genius, of course, is that it is now no longer an individual thing but it is a matter of involving everyone of our backs, and the wings are now able to run well because of the use of an attacking full-back.

The wingers' involvement in defence was also very important to our success. If you are going to counter-attack, the threequarters must get back to support the full-back, and by practising this constantly, we found that it not only helped our counter-attacking, but it improved our cover defence enormously. I think this was why we won the first Test.

Q. *What do you look for in players?*

A. One takes fitness for granted. You expect people at this level to be fit. In the actual selection of players, I think that character is one of the most important things. As we had a year to pick the side, obviously I had a fair idea of who would be selected and who would not. I made a point of speaking to these boys. I knew that I would not get to know some of them terribly well, but at least I would get some idea of their mental make-up. This is important because the more I coach the more I think of the importance of psychology. It plays a great part in the coaching of rugby football because players must believe in themselves. Once players believe in themselves then you are 90% of the way there. If they have character, they have guts, they have courage. Anybody who thinks he can go through a tour of New Zealand without guts might as well stay at home. He is not for a tour of that kind. He must have guts, he must have character, he must have the will to win.

Probably we were lucky that six of our players had been to New Zealand in 1966 and a number of the boys, the Welsh boys, had been with the Welsh team out there in 1969. They had been on the receiving end on so many occasions and there was a determination on the part of these fellows to do well. This determination was trans-ferred to some of the younger players who were on tour, and when you have your older people on tour prepared to train hard, to show by example, then obviously the others will carry on from there.

Thirdly, of course, there was a great deal of skill in the team. We were very fortunate in that respect. We had them in the forwards. We had the scrummaging skill of Ray McLoughlin, of Sean Lynch, of Sandy Carmichael and of Ian McLauchlan and "Stack" Stevens, so the corner-stone was there.

In the backs as well, we had players of experience and of skill. Now, there is no point in my going through the backs, because probably they were as skilful as any Lions side that has ever gone out. One remembers the great side of 1955. There was so much skill in the 1959 side as well. It is a recurring factor in Lions' rugby. On this occasion, that skill was allied to the character of the forwards that we sent out, and above everything else, to players who believed in themselves and knew that they could do well.

Q. *What training programme did you adopt in Eastbourne?*

A. In the first instance, I had to find out how fit they were, but I also tried to give them a little pride in the fact that they were Lions.

We were very fortunate that the Four Home Unions committee had provided us with very smart track suits. If I said, "We shall start our training at ten minutes pastten," we started training at ten minutes past ten. We went out together.

Before going out, I would tell them exactly what we proposed to do, and we kept to this pattern for the whole tour. Players were invited to submit their views. Beforehand, if I knew that one man possibly had more to offer than another, I would take him aside and discuss this point with him, knowing that he would be relating these things to the rest of the party in the morning. I wanted to be conversant with any new thinking, or with any contribution that an individual had.

Q. *How much importance did you attach to them all turning out in a red track suit?*

A. Very important. If the side looks good, then the possibility is that it may well BE good. Make no bones about this at all. I also told them before each session, "Some of you will be playing in red shirts, others will be playing in white shirts." And I asked them in a letter to bring a red shirt and a white shirt with them on tour. What is the point of sixteen forwards coming out dressed in the colours of the Quins, Coventry, Northampton and what have you, and nobody knows who's playing for what side?

Initially, I used to do the warm-ups myself - I'm not a P.E. man, and not qualified as such, but I've done a bit of coaching and was capable of doing a warm-up. None-the-less, there were lots of players who were trained in Physical Education and I would ask them to take the warm-up session for me.

I might warn the player of this the night before, or I might warn him before breakfast, or I might warn him after breakfast! It depended very much on the make-up of the individual. If he was a worrier, I wouldn't tell him the night before, I would probably tell him after breakfast: I wouldn't want to spoil his breakfast for him.

The extrovert type, who had a great thrill in doing this, well, I would give him the pleasure of telling him about it the night before, and he could work it out. This gave me an added advantage because while the group was warming up in an extended session of a quarter of an hour or twenty minutes, I could take one player out and give him individual attention. I found this particularly useful. You never had enough time, really, to give attention to the individual in your squad. Sometimes I took two players or three players - it all depended.

After we had warmed-up, I used to do a number of skills, I might arrange six lines of five players. The first line would pass the ball out in three-quarter formation, and then when it had reached the last man, you would get on to your skill. The skill might have been that last man to take it would run like mad, put the ball down and then possibly the first man would take the ball.

In other words the inside player would be the next man to pick up this ball off the deck. He would pick it up, he would run, he would put it down, and then the next man take it. They would do this in the round. They might do this two or three times, and it is very hard work.

Then perhaps I would make each member of each team fall with the ball in turn, and as they fell they would pop this ball up. There would have to be support, there would have to be continuity and, of course, as far as fitness was concerned, it was ideal. They would cover a lot of ground at top speed.

You could always relate this to something important that you would do later on, say with the backs or with the forwards. For instance you could say, "Right shoulder down the line, ball on the trailing hip." So now your sup-port would have to be much closer, and you would do this a number of times; five times round the field, six times round the field. Not round the field really but in the round, the round being a circle of about sixty yards diameter. This way the backs would learn what sort of body attitude was helpful in the ruck situation. We never did the same ploys on successive days; this lent a certain amount of variation.

After that came the major part of the coaching session. This concerned individual skills, where I put players in different parts of the field. For instance the halves would work together. The wings might have been deployed in a straight line just throwing the ball a fair distance, or throwing the ball in from touch. The full-backs may have been working together, I might have put the back rows in a corner of the field, working out back-row moves. The point was that they were all doing skills which were related to their own particular game. This meant that there could never be an excuse. If I called for a back row move, no back row forward could turn round to me and say, "We haven't worked out any moves."

Coaching in individual skills is only of value when it is

related to game situations. Anything one does in a coaching session has to be related to game situations. Therefore one has to work out meticulously what one does in a particular session.

Having done that, we came to the meat of the session. This of course concerned the unit skills.

On the Monday and the Thursday, we did scrummaging. This was followed by ruck situations, and I would try to set up ways of making the rucks as lively as possible and related as near to the game situation as possible - always bearing in mind, of course that I didn't want people to get hurt. It is so important to have a touring party who know exactly what your aims are. You mustn't have a silly fool amongst them who is going to try and maim one of your own team. I have seen it happen in club sessions - possibly two people in contention for the same place, or one chap has got it in for another chap, and they are silly. They must use the ultimate in self-discipline. Whether they hold a grudge or whether they don't, they must not go out of their way to hurt someone, just because they've been hurt a bit themselves or because a chap has put his shoulder in fairly hard. He's only doing it for the good of the cause.

With the unit skills, the difficulty is that you spend thirty or forty minutes scrummaging and ten minutes on your rucking, you have forty or fifty minutes when your backs have got to be doing something as well. Now, I was lucky to have people like John Dawes and Doug Smith to help here. The problem is how can you possibly employ backs for this length of time. You can only possibly run them for ten minutes or a quarter of an hour at top speed. I didn't want them to run at half pace, because if they run at half pace in training they are going to run at half-pace in a game, so they can only do top stuff for about ten minutes. Therefore, for the rest of the time I got them to work out game situations, possibly static, where they had to make a quick transference of the ball from one player to another. I used to observe this occasionally and some-times take it myself. Line up six players in a line, another six players in a line, and get them to move theball swiftly from one end of the line to the other. Have them compete against the clock or against one another. It did mean fingertip passing and it did help them with their skills. There were a number of other things that they could do. We'd set them up in such a way and throw a high ball that the full-back could take facing the nearest touch line, and then everybody in turn would take it upon himself to link up with the full-back. Backs would have to go back to a position where they could set up a counter-attack.

There were so many other interesting things that could be done. If you asked Barry John what he would prefer to do, he would probably say, "Play 10 minutes of soccer." I have nothing against ten minutes of soccer. It was very good for them. It kept their minds alert especially since they could not, as I have said, keep running at top speed. If was far better for them to be employed doing some-thing that was of interest to them and keeping their minds active.

Having done the unit skill session, we then had a semi-opposed session. In this, I liked to have the team for the next match all wearing the same coloured shirts. Then I'd say, "Reds, all of you on that side." Usually I allowed them to play with the elements, with the sun, with the wind, because it is important to have a nice dress rehearsal. Then I'd ask the others to form a pack to be in opposition. I would send the other backs away to do some individual skills that they wanted to do, and I would carry that game on as long as I felt it was lively and interesting to them. I tried to bring in the things that I had done earlier in my session.

If it was, for instance, a counter-attacking session, we did a great deal of counter-attacking. If it was covering in depth, then we'd do a lot of covering in depth. If we paid particular attention to the short penalty, then we'd have a number of those. One tried to make it as much of a game situation as one possibly could.

It is important to have opposition at training sessions because then you can call for scrummages, you can call for line-outs, you can call for back row moves. The All Blacks did not do them. For most of their sessions they had fifteen men versus the coach. To me this is absolute heresy, absolute rubbish. I wouldn't have it. Another pack is essential.

Q. Was there any stage when you used pure un-opposed rugby for fifteen men?

A.   No I always used some kind of opposition; when forwards were injured I would even put backs in the pack to make up the numbers.

Q. Did you have opposition in the lineout practice?

A.   Oh, yes! I tried to make it as realistic as possible.

Q. Did you have tackling as well?

A.   A certain amount, but not too much.

Finally, after we had done that semi-opposed session, we finished off with perhaps some weight training. Ray McLoughlin is a great believer in this, and I would allow him to take this particular session. Then I always had my last pound of flesh by making them all sprint, say four or five sprints - 25 yards - then I'd make it 40, then 50. Then perhaps I would push it up to 70 yards and I might finish off with 100. It was an important part of the work, but I did emphasise to all the players, "Now, look, if you feel you are going to pull a hamstring or something, get off the paddock. I don't want you. You know whether you are good enough to do this or not. Don't come to me afterwards and say that you have pulled a hamstring. It is up to you to make absolutely certain that you can take it."

That was the way I did it. The whole session lasted two hours but eventually I was able to condense it into about an hour and a half. I felt, initially, that I needed my two hours. People watching in New Zealand thought it was all very gentle, but when you added it all up, we did a fair amount of work it was all related to game situations in rugby football. That was the important thing.